Masculine/Feminine

POST-CONTEMPORARY INTERVENTIONS

Series Editors: Stanley Fish and Fredric Jameson

———

LATIN AMERICA IN TRANSLATION/

EN TRADUCCIÓN/EM TRADUÇÃO

Masculine/Feminine

Practices of Difference(s)

NELLY RICHARD

Silvia R. Tandeciarz and Alice A. Nelson, Translators

DUKE UNIVERSITY PRESS Durham & London 2004

© 2004 Duke University Press

Printed in the United States of

America on acid-free paper ⊗

Designed by Amy Ruth Buchanan

Typeset in Quadraat by Tseng

Information Systems, Inc.

Library of Congress Cataloging-in-

Publication Data appear on the last

printed page of this book.

Contents

Translators' Acknowledgments

We relied on the expertise of many individuals in the completion of this translation, and to them we would like to extend our sincere gratitude. Kathleen Ross, John French, Juan Poblete, Alberto Moreiras, Greg Mullins, Patrick Hub, and Pablo Yáñez all offered valuable feedback and encouragement at critical points in the process. The superb editorial work of J. Reynolds Smith, Sharon P. Torian, Kate Lothman, and Leigh Anne Couch strengthened the manuscript, and their patience through several unfortunate delays helped us bring the project to fruition. Our home institutions, the College of William and Mary and the Evergreen State College, gave us crucial research support and facilities to complete the project. And without the support of our families — Pablo, Ximena, Cristóbal, Patrick — none of this would have been possible. Finally, we are grateful for the trust Nelly Richard placed in us; we hope our rendering of her work into English will help us convey our deepest appreciation.

Translators' Preface

Nelly Richard figures among the most prominent cultural critics writing in Latin America today. As part of the Chilean neo–avant-garde that emerged during the Pinochet dictatorship (1973–90), Richard worked to expand and deepen the possibilities for cultural debate within that constrained context and has continued to offer incisive cultural commentary about the country's transition to democracy. Richard's rigorous essays and books engage questions of Latin American identity within the context of North/South debates on postmodernism and neoliberalism, with a strong emphasis on gender analysis and micropolitical strategies of resistance. Well known as the founder and director of the influential *Revista de crítica cultural* (Santiago, Chile), Richard has been central to the dissemination throughout Latin America of work by key contemporary thinkers, including Beatriz Sarlo, Néstor García Canclini, Jacques Derrida, Ernesto Laclau, Fredric Jameson, Jesús Martín Barbero, and Diamela Eltit. Like Richard's own essays, the *Revista* has put into dialogue theoretical perspectives from Latin America, Europe, and the United States, creating a lively forum for intellectual debate on culture, theory, and politics since its founding in 1990.[1]

Born in France, Richard completed her degree in literature at the Sorbonne and moved to Chile in 1970, a year characterized by the euphoric victory of Unidad Popular (Popular Unity) under the leadership of the democratically elected socialist president Salvador Allende. During the Popular Unity period, Richard served as coordinator of art exhibitions for the Museo de Bellas Artes in Santiago, a post that she abandoned after the violent overthrow of Allende in 1973. Under the Pinochet dictatorship, Richard became involved with unofficial art circuits, aligning herself within the margins of opposition to the military regime, as both a protagonist and an analyst of the neo–avant-garde (or *avanzada*) cultural scene. The essays in this book bear traces of that time, whether in Richard's emphasis on alternative artists and art movements such as CADA (*Colectivo de Acciones de Arte* [Art Actions Collective]), or in her piecing together fragments of art history and criticism first circulated precariously as photocopies under the military regime.

Richard was also closely connected to the feminist movement reconstituted slowly in various pockets throughout the country. Although many of those engaged in oppositional activities from the beginning of the Pinochet years were women, a feminist movement only received public acknowledgment as such after the eruption of massive national protests in 1983–84. As Julieta Kirkwood and other Chilean feminists noted, the ways in which power operated under the military regime had made feminist analysis not only particularly relevant but also politically necessary. In 1987, Richard served as one of the main organizers of what would prove to be the most significant literary event under the dictatorship—indeed, one of the most important in all of Latin America during the 1980s—the Primer Congreso de Literatura Femenina Latinoamericana (First International Conference on Latin American Women's Literature), held in Santiago in August of that year. As is evident in *Escribir en los bordes*, a published collection of essays from the conference, this gathering raised questions of difference and institutional exclusions faced by women writers and resituated debates on *écriture féminine* within particularly Latin American cultural coordinates. Richard's *Masculino/femenino*, published in 1993, revisits key questions from this conference, reconsidering them in light of Chile's return to democracy.

Like *Masculino/femenino*, Richard's other collections—particularly *La estratificación de los márgenes* (1989), *La insubordinación de los signos* (1994), and *Residuos y metáforas* (1998)—have insisted on micropractices of difference and an aesthetic of the fragmentary, partial, and oblique as opening new discursive and artistic possibilities for contesting hegemonic discourses. Her own challenging, suggestive prose style underscores this stance and resonates with the neo-avant-garde impulse of writers like Diamela Eltit. Situated at the intersections of literary criticism, art history, aesthetics, philosophy, and feminist theory, Richard's work seeks to illuminate the complex relationships between institutional and contestatory discourses, between legitimized and marginalized practices, and between established social identities and subjectivities in crisis. And, far from seeing her work as completed with democracy's return, she has insisted that the consensus-driven Chilean transition has necessitated a renewed commitment to debate. As Richard writes in *Residuos y metáforas*: "I think it is necessary to defend the secret of these opacities and refractions against the linguistic tyranny of the simple, direct, and transparent discourse characterizing today's social communications, which have left language without narrative twists, without poetic turns of double and ambiguous meanings."[2] In the context of the Chilean democracy's suppressed contradictions, Richard contends that cultural criticism should "make readers suspicious of the false assumption that forms are innocent and languages transparent, an assumption hiding the fact that pacts and agreements of shared interests tacitly restrain [other] values, meanings, and forms of power."[3] Critical writing, she asserts, should inspire readers to "break the mold of prefabricated meaning."[4]

Clearly interdisciplinary, Richard's critical practice is distinguished by her sustained focus on the margins, borders, and interstices of cultural expression as those sites illuminating the most salient social conflicts—questions of power and exclusion—and bearing traces of desire, including those for social change. While one could subsume her work under the label of *cultural studies*, she herself designates it as *cultural criticism* or *cultural critique*, a distinction that has garnered its own academic following, both through Richard's seminars at the alternative university ARCIS in Santiago and through the *Revista de crítica cultural*. As Ana del Sarto explains it, "Cultural Critique construes its locus from aesthetic materiality, in order to 'critically transform the real' . . . while Cultural Studies construes it from social materiality, in order critically to produce social reality."[5] While the differences between these two forms of cultural practice have led to healthy philosophical debates, what we would like to stress here is not so much the usefulness or validity of one over the other, but rather Richard's own sense of alterity vis-à-vis dominant discourses and the historical conditions in which her work is embedded.[6]

Taken as a body of work, then, Richard's essays have proven instrumental in reclaiming so-called high art (or avant-garde aesthetic practices) for a progressive political project of institutional, cultural, economic, and social critique—a claim particularly significant in the face of the traditional left's historical rejection of such aesthetically oriented practices as complicit with bourgeois or statist interests. In this regard, Richard's work resonates strongly in a U.S. academic context shaken by the advent of cultural studies, a context marked by struggles to reconcile old disciplinary perspectives emphasizing aesthetics with interdisciplinary approaches to culture broadly defined as the practice of everyday life. Paradoxically positioned between tradition and innovation, Richard is one of the few contemporary critics to successfully bridge literary criticism and aesthetic critique, visual arts and narrative, social practices and representation.

While Richard's practice emerged in a specific local register, and insistently positions itself within the Chilean and Latin American contexts, we are convinced that through a sustained commitment to translation, her local observations will have a decisive impact on the global cultural field.[7] We hope that "this analysis, as its bond to another culture is rendered more explicit, will only be assisted in leading readers to uncover for themselves, in their own situation, their own tactics, their own creations, and their own initiatives."[8] We hope that our renderings of Nelly Richard's essays not only conserve the rigor of her prose but also stimulate English-speaking readers to accept her challenge to engage meaningfully in their own cultural critiques.

Note on This Translation

Throughout the text, words in quotation marks or italics follow the author's usage in the original Spanish. In a few instances we have included terms from the Spanish language original, italicized and in brackets after our English translation, in order to convey further nuance for readers of Spanish.

Richard quotes from a range of sources, mostly in the Spanish original or in Spanish translation. When these quotes were available in English translation, we used the standard published versions and referenced them in the bibliography in place of the Spanish. When translations were not available, we translated the extracts ourselves. The bibliography contains only those works cited by Richard herself, and not those referenced by the translators in the preface and notes. Likewise, in order to conserve Richard's original endnote numbers, translators' notes are indicated by typographic symbols rather than numbers in the text.

In some cases bibliographic citations in the original text were incomplete; we have remedied this whenever possible. For information on the sources originally quoted by the author, please refer to the Spanish language edition of this work.

ONE

Spatial Politics: Cultural Criticism
and Feminist Theory

The forms through which culture speaks using words and images —
the systems of signs that communicate culture and the webs of messages that socially transmit it — embody and defend interests prejudi-
cially linked to certain hegemonic representations, reinforcing lines
of power, dominance, and authority.

Cultural ideologies render invisible (*naturalize*) the constructions
and mediations of signs, making us believe that words and images
speak for themselves rather than for the interposed and concerted
voices of the social discourses historically plotting their meanings.
The first gesture of critical resistance to the false assumption of
signs' neutrality, then, is to expose the codes that erase cultural ideologies' signifying work.

Cultural criticism functions precisely by revealing the imbrication
of the parts and interlocking gears that make discursive mechanisms
function. It works by demonstrating that they all are moveable and
interchangeable, and that — contrary to what is decreed by the im-
mobilizing and demobilizing weight of traditions and conventions
tied to the defense of the status quo's integrity — the voices of these
discourses can be altered and replaced. Cultural criticism seeks to
suspend the sentence that condemns signs to remaining static or
routine; instead it propagates the microzones of agitation and com-
motion that unsettle the normative equilibrium of what is dictated by
habit or convenience, and thereby creates disturbances in the semiotic organization of messages that produce and reproduce institu-

tional consent. This criticism uses the sociocommunicative materiality of signs as a stage from which to question and intervene in the modalities of discourse, both the representations of power and the powers of representation. In Barbero's words: "It is not only a matter of power utilizing discourse as weapon, sophism, or blackmail, but rather of discourse forming an integral part of the plot of violence, control, and struggle that constitutes the practice of power."[1]

In order to dismantle these forms of power, cultural criticism fixes its gaze on those deviating practices, on those movements in open dispute with tendencies legitimated by the conformist and recuperative vocabularies of academic fetishism, of aesthetic commercialism or political ideologism. The task of cultural criticism—which reaps its reflexive and combative energy from the struggles of alternative practices to configure the emergent dynamics of the new—is to empower the destabilizing effects of conflicting codes and representations emerging, in linguistic rebellion, from new sociocultural subjectivities.[2]

Another task of this criticism is the antihegemonic struggle against the division and parceling out of cultural power. This power follows multiple paths—traced by imposed or negotiated boundaries—that survey and cross diverse maps of identity and social thought: demarcating territories, establishing checkpoints and zones of influence that regulate the system's borders as a place from which to debate the tension of limits that include or exclude. That absorb or discard, award or punish, depending on the types of practices in question. And depending on whether these practices attempt only to reconfirm what already has been agreed on by official culture or whether they audaciously attempt to deregulate this agreement of established forms, bringing into conflict the dominant pacts of signification that unilaterally regulate values, signs, and forms of power.

The limits of inclusion and exclusion territorializing the boundaries of institutional control are neither fixed nor linear. These limits

—fractured at multiple and variable points of intersection and flight —contemplate zones of greater or lesser programmatic density, of more or less flexible transit. Various forces of social and cultural change can exert sectorial or regional pressure on these limits—in order to move them, partially relax their marks of closure and vigilance, weaken rigidities, and locally defeat their resistances. Among them are: (1) forces protagonized by new groups of actors (youth, women, indigenous peoples, homosexuals, etc.) who emerge from the multiplicity of the social to reclaim their right to single out difference against the repressive uniformity of the majority's standard of identity; (2) forces invigorated by the feminist debate denouncing the homological foreclosure of masculine self-representation; and (3) transcultural and multicultural forces of the Latin American periphery that revise and critique the metropolitan synthesis of the center's modernity, and so on.

A review of the post-coup Chilean cultural context and of the democratic transition can help foreground some of the effects (and the putting into effect) of practices registering the impulse of these new critical forces that are transforming the fields of artistic and cultural thought. The transformations of cultural imaginaries stimulated by such practices, however, do not yet appear to have been incorporated into the democratic culture's horizon of debates.

Critical Junctures in the Chilean Cultural Debate

The articulation of a space for public debate—that is to say, a space in which ideas acquire their greatest consistency and polemical vigor, their greatest capacity for intellectual impact—depends on multiple factors that put into play a plurality of sociocultural mechanisms, all of them wounded by the experience of the dictatorship. The destructuring of practices' socialization networks and the confinement of voices to the microcircuits of a fragmentary public isolated and separated groups from each other, blocking the exchange between works and the structures for their reception that would have helped to expand and diversify the range and registers of their reading.

The democratic transition put an end to the prohibitions and restrictions of the "culture of fear." But cultural debates have not, as a consequence, regained their meaningfulness. The reopening of public venues for cultural intervention (the press, television, the university, government ministries, etc.), has made clear instead that the dominant tendency—with certain exceptions confirming the rule—consists of celebrating the complacent symbolism of a triple mandate: *massiveness* (to evaluate participation according to merely quantitative criteria); *monumentalism* (to saturate performative facades with visibility and presence so as to dissipate the nuanced ambiguity of critical and reflective interstices); *pluralism* (to court plurality, bringing together the greatest diversity of opinions, but taking care that this confrontation of tendencies does not disrupt the passivity of the whole).

The creation and defense of spaces for debate depend, in turn, on improving those conditions that have completely devalued culture and cultural reflection. Manifestations of cultural reflection today are victims of a meager amount of attention that punishes its critical proposals and separates its polemics from the movement of ideas animating the public sphere. Television and the press saturate the numerous stages dedicated to political conversation with redundancies and predictability: the same adversaries, the same disputes, the same clichés circularly remitted and transmitted by media that increasingly trivialize the distance between news items and editorials. Lacking sufficient imagination to overcome the narrowness and banality of the simply conjunctural themes driven by an agenda of consent, these spaces generally reveal themselves to be incapable of venturing any connections that respond to the political-intellectual challenge of reexamining the links between "culture," "politics," and "democracy," connections both more conceptually rigorous and less bureaucratically and administratively accommodating.

This incapacity is inscribed, in turn, in the more global frame of profound disincentives with respect to the dialogue between culture and politics—a dialogue that almost always has proven in vain, no matter what sector has proposed it. While the role of forging an aristocratic vision of culture has corresponded historically to the conservative thought of the right (culture as the cultivation of spiritual values expressing class privilege), that vision greatly exceeds the right's political representation, imbuing prevailing notions and categories in many of the social definitions of culture orienting us daily. Definitions traditionally linked to what certain Sunday supplements (like that of the newspaper El Mercurio) call "Arts and Letters," with all the sublimated charge of a transcendent-idealistic conception of culture as the superior and universal expression of a refined individuality. The most widely disseminated images in the press and on television today, of the creator and of aesthetic rituals as contemplative and disinterested experiences, continue to emphasize this dematerialized vision of culture, according to which artists and writers fetishistically embody an *excess* of sensibility and imagination. An *excess* exalted in works that seem to transcend clashes of interests and ideological antagonism, as if culture were not a sociomaterial process whose productive and communicative textures relate bodies, signs, and institutions in struggles of economies, languages, and desires.

If we shift our gaze toward the forms the traditional left has used to interpret culture, partisan instrumentalism and ideological reductionism come into view as recurrent distortions in artistic practice, exacerbated in those contexts where political art had to be dramatized to protest and denounce the dictatorship. Instrumentalism and reductionism due to the assumption that the calling of artistic production is to represent or illustrate (in a subordinate manner) social tensions, as if those tensions consisted of preconfigured meanings and not the process in which the work *intervenes* (disorganizes, reformulates) through an active and multisignifying play of replicas, disjunctures, and contradictory proposals.

Despite the new left's rejection of militant art's gross partisan functionalism, it continues for the most part to uphold a conception of culture that posits it as a kind of symbolic-expressive supplement capable of *transfiguring* social conflicts *into images*, but without sufficient protagonism to *dismantle and recodify its figurations and significations.*

Various political interventions forming part of the socialist debate[3] call for the incorporation of "the cultural" into democratic thought as a new dimension open to the theme of (individual and collective) *subjectivity*, one of the themes repressed by the overly economistic dogma of the Marxist left. A theme that today invites the exercise of sensibility and imagination in the creative design of lifestyles and forms of cohabitation which revitalize the experience of the city and the neighborhood, the environment, free time, interpersonal relationships, and the like.

New socialism's debates recognize the erosion of politics' traditional representations and meanings, heretofore organized around the identification of power as a centralized referent in the form of the State; and around the discussion of strategies for battle, conquest, and the exercise of that power seen simply as questions of institutional governability. The erosion of these petrified motifs in the classic left's doctrinaire versions suggests, in contrast, that only a more *cultural* dimension of the social problematic could recapture the political imagination. A dimension articulating "struggles of interest" (struggles vindicating rights) but also combining "struggles of desires" (that is, struggles expressing options for symbolic change that seek to rediagram every detail of daily life). Part of the new democratic scheme is based on the fact that social and communal heterogeneity has led to the formation of sectorally segregated groups, whose liberatory utopias clash not only with "exploitative" relationships (in the economistic language of class struggle) but also with "oppressive" and "dominating" (sexually, racially, etc.) relationships, following a transversality of forms of power that interweave multiple chains of subjection, impossible to untangle with a single (central) paradigm for resolving conflict.[4]

The theoretical reorientations of international socialist debates around these new figures of the left's political-cultural imaginary have influenced local positions: those linked to Socialist Renewal (Renovación Socialista) sectors played a decisive leadership role in the Chilean process of democratic reorganization. Nevertheless, the attention such sectors directed toward the Chilean artistic and cultural scene—whose rearticulation paralleled its own discussion of the political crisis of representation in the eighties—for the most part failed to appreciate the transformative potential of the critical energy contained in the work of ideological and cultural derepresentation practiced by that "new scene."[5] Despite the fact that related referents (postmarxism in the social sciences, poststructuralism in artistic and cultural theory) could have promised a complicitous dialogue regarding the transformation of languages carried out in unofficial culture by its most heterodox tendencies, that dialogue did not occur, or only occurred in a fragmentary fashion.[6]

Most sociologists of alternative culture utilized research frameworks oriented toward criteria of social performance, whose logic of efficiency proved hostile to the oppositional impulse of artistic practices whose intensity could not be channeled through the rationalist-pragmatic terms of social scientific discourse. Insofar as that discourse was financed by international agencies expecting useful observations about the sociopolitical dynamics of the re/constitution of subjects destined to form the new set of actors who would lead the democratic transition, it could not account for the characteristic uselessness of the most perturbing aesthetics of the moment, which sought to exacerbate words and images as zones for disordering signs.[7] The political-libidinal excesses of those aesthetics, which twisted codes and identities through languages refracting the ideological functionalism of militant art, were ignored by most sociology of alternative culture and also by most Socialist Renewal intellectuals. It is curious to see how, today, socialism's theoretical and political agenda seeks to dialogue with postmodernism (heterogeneity, fragmentation, multiplicity, decentering, etc.), given its earlier inability to recognize that all this heterological emphasis placed on the multiversity of meaning was already being conjugated in the critical deconstructionism of a theoretical and cultural scene opting for syntactic rupture over militant phraseology, transcultural parody over

Latin Americanist dogma, a microbiographical vocabulary over the historicist epic.

One of the most lively debates to emerge from this scene relates to the theme of gender-sexual difference and identity. Formulated through the relationship between women and culture, this debate was articulated in the dialogue between cultural criticism and feminist theory.

Language, Knowledge, Theory, and Culture: The Feminist Intervention

Feminism in Chile achieved its most historic dimension from the *women's movements* that served as platforms for civic vindication and social and political mobilization, introducing the problematic of gender into the socialist debate during the years of democratic reconstruction. The problematic of the specificity of women and the non-subordination of their particular demands was formulated through the coordinates of gender identity, understood not only as a vector of struggle against male oppression and discrimination (symbolized by the feminist slogan of the last years of the military regime: "Democracy in the nation and in the home") but also as an axis for questioning traditional ways of thinking and acting politically in the face of new theoretical intersections and interventions (for example, "the personal is also political").[8]

The process for articulating theoretical reflections on women during the period of the dictatorship was shaped by women researchers (sociologists, historians, anthropologists, etc.) who defined a feminist way of thinking most rigorously and creatively expressed in the work of Julieta Kirkwood.[9] This way of thinking—emphasizing political-feminist analysis (aimed at strengthening feminism as a social movement) and elaborated from the social sciences—never engaged, or barely did, the critical reflections that were simultaneously developing a thematics of the "feminine"—of what is considered "minority"—around the symbolic discourses and cultural imaginaries deployed by unofficial art and culture during the military period.[10] Social science research tended, rather, to reinscribe the division between the rational-productive (science) and the irrational (art), positing aesthetic production as ornamental and therefore disconnected from questions regarding the processes through which artistic representations and symbols weave together and unravel—with their *forms* and *styles*—the sheer volume of cultural ideologies. In other words, while they expressed a "sociology critical of women's condition,"[11] they tended to ignore the importance for feminism of theoretical reflection regarding discursive and signifying modes, despite the fact that it is precisely these modes that give material density (both enunciative and communicative) to the categories of social thought structuring representations of gender and identity. On the other hand, theoretical reflection regarding art and literature also failed to connect with wider sectors of cultural debate which could have lent critical strength to its new proposals for reading and analysis—proposals indicating how marks of the masculine or of the feminine articulate cultural discourse and are disarticulated/rearticulated by artistic languages, enabling the nonconformity of a subjectivity in crisis.

These situations, once limited by the lack of intercommunication, today show signs of changing due to the increasing public exposure of the subject of women, which makes it resonate more broadly in a range of collective venues.

In the case of women's literature and feminist literary criticism, this change derives from an important Congreso de Literatura Femenina Latinoamericana [International Conference on Latin American Women's Literature] (Santiago, Chile, 1987) "that created networks through the mass media for staging a public reflection and discourse about women's writing and its social and historical significance."[12] In the case of social research on women's practices (that until then had taken place "outside universities, in alternative academic centers, in nongovernmental organizations [NGOs]"),[13] this change signals how "in the last two years, through traditional universities' extension centers, a few isolated courses related to women's issues have begun to be offered, and some university-based academics have recently introduced gender issues into their more specialized courses."[14]

These relatively new formats for intervention (in the national press, the university, etc.) need to be evaluated in light of the challenges they pose to feminist theory and gender practices, the new rubs and frictions generated by the gap between the promise of a collective female "we" ["*nosotras*"], and the multiple, crisscrossing discourses of public culture. These rubs and frictions generate different problem areas, many of them intersecting with major theoretical nodes of feminist practice. I signal three of them here:

1. The binary us/them (a female "we" versus "the others"): The feminism in which "women join together who want to strengthen each other in the move toward a better self-image and the constitution of strong and autonomous subjects,"[15] condenses in a female "we" its first gesture of solidarity, reaffirmation, and self-expression. If that gesture is indeed necessary for consolidating the feeling of a gender-based community—always vulnerable to the monumental rhetorical armature of the sociomasculine consensus—feminism must also learn to deconstruct the closure/enclosure of that female "we" in order to inflect its mark as a *plural* staging of interventions and confrontations between identities, genders, sexes, cultures, languages, and forms of power. This gesture needs to be made plural so as to communicate rather than isolate. And its critique of the dominant masculine model of identity must be related to other critiques, to authoritarian and totalitarian conceptions of the subject, so that all together they might weave liberating alliances in favor of a collective, fluid, and *multiple* subjectivity.

2. Power/knowledge and strategy: Having disproved and dismantled the artifice that knowledge and theory are the (supposedly) neutral instruments of a presumably universal, logical, and scientific rationality; and having demonstrated that these instruments traditionally have been employed to reinforce the masculinization of knowledge: what more does feminist theory intend? To oppose that masculine

way of knowing by contesting it frontally and en masse from that "other" feminine way of knowing, rescued from censure and held up as *separate*? Or rather, to subvert the dominant way of knowing by creating oblique interferences that deprogram its enunciations *from within*?

3. Disciplines and paradigms of knowledge: The incorporation of a specialized dimension of women's issues (as thematic supplement/complement) to the field of academic knowledge as currently organized will not suffice to undo the androcentric paradigm of knowledge—based on the false assumption of science or theory's neutrality and universality—that governs the disciplines.[16] How can feminist criticism become a *deterritorializing* force that can alter the composition and distribution of academic knowledge, outside the institutionalized preserve of "Women's Studies"?

These difficulties regarding strategies for the public exposition and intervention of women's issues are undoubtedly responsible for complicating the paths for communication between feminist reflection and the cultural circuits of the democratic transition—complications and barriers defining a situation in which it appears that feminism and "its discourses continue unsupported to generate debate on the cultural and literary scene. As a counterpoint, women themselves tend toward isolation in their search to construct a history, traditions, and intertextuality between generically equal products in a field of inequalities."[17]

The problem areas signaled here are linked to various crucial questions for feminist thought, posed by Rossana Rossanda in the following terms:

Have women produced a culture of their own, a specific, previously repressed or submerged way of knowing that, upon emerging, would contribute a substantial correction and not simply an "addition" to culture as it has existed up to now? In sum, have women produced a different mode of being? . . . What critique of knowledge reveals the masculinity of knowledge? What other demystifying reading does it anticipate? And if culture is not solely a depository of various notions, but rather a system of relationships between history and the present, between the present and the present, a world of people and values, what does the feminine invest in this culture of dominators and oppressors, how does it subvert it, and what different relational systems does it suggest?[18]

These questions intersect with another question: Is it valid for women to construct an identity based on the notion that the masculine-dominant's "other" is the "proper" realm of the feminine? Might it not be instead that what is "proper" to the feminine is the tension-filled, reformulating product of the cross between mechanisms of appropriation/misappropriation/counterappropriation that the dominating and the dominated confront in the interior of a culture whose registers of (hegemonic) power and resistance (subalternity) are always *intertwined*?

We already know that language does more than name. By naming, it defines and categorizes: each name carves out a fraction of reality and experience to which language gives a logical-conceptual statute according to the rationalizing scheme culture legitimates as dominant. We also know that this model is necessarily patriarchal because civilization's rationality worked for centuries to assimilate the masculine to the transcendental and universal. Philosophical constructs and cultural-symbolic formations are based on the fraudulent montage that decided to grant the advantage to the masculine via an association with the abstract-general and to disadvantage the feminine via an association with the concrete-particular. How do women respond to this newfound awareness that their entry into the worlds of culture is *mediated* by a language whose masculine-hegemonic interests work against their independence as speaking subjects?

An initial response to emerge from radical feminism is a refusal to play the game: women must refuse to speak while intercepted by the rationalizing mechanisms of male domination. Therefore they must reject those instruments most identified with the hypermasculinity of the Logos (philosophical totalities, scientific abstraction, theoretical systematization, etc.) because they all serve masculine codifications of power. That same radical feminism promotes, as a way out, rescuing those forms of expression and communication considered "feminine," that is, free from masculine-conceptual reticulation: linguistic forms more intuitive than logical, more material than conceptual, more affective than rational, more aesthetic than operational, more confessional than declamatory, and so on. All of these forms supposedly reveal a *purely* feminine way of knowing: a pure knowledge of the feminine, a knowledge of *pure* femininity (divested of the masculine), deposited in a women's culture as separate and autonomous. This value of purity, which many feminists seek to recover as a value constitutive of an *integral* femininity, would entail cleansing culture of all contamination by masculine signs despoiling it in order to reach that which is "proper" to women: that which is exclusively female. But does it make sense to reiterate tautologically as feminine those same values (sensibility, corporeality, affectivity, etc.) that the dominant gender ideology has already marked as such in order to segregate them to the margins of historical-social rationality? Are not these the same categories imposed by domination that are being postulated as categories resistant to domination? Don't they adhere to the same system that reproduces gender dichotomies, recreating (with an inverted sign) the same masculine/feminine difference newly frozen in opposition and exclusion? How valid is it to imagine a *pure* culture as the utopian horizon of a place, just short of, or just beyond, patriarchy: a culture entirely purged of hostile or contaminating sediments?

Women's history and culture were never pieced together *outside* male domination and colonization. Their forms always intermixed with those of the system of authority in whose interstices and fissures they practiced disobedience. Extracting the feminine from the field of replies and counterreplies (domination, consent, resistance, confrontation, etc.) in which this category always negotiated and renegotiated the limits of its identity and oppositionality is equivalent to excising it from one of its most dynamic tensions: one that responds to the realization that masculine domination is not a fixed discourse but rather a discourse whose enunciations are historically and contextually driven and reformulated according to changing rules that inform sequences of always mobile clashes.

On the other hand, cultural discourse is a field of forms of power and significations that come into practice through the deployment of multidirectional forces. The signs that make up language are depositories of memory intermixing various registers of struggle between ideological-cultural interests.[19] Masculine and feminine play an active role in these controversies that render signs polemical, battlefields in the production of meaning. To empty a sign of the content built into its interior by one of the two forces in struggle (the masculine) not only has the memory-stripping effect of depriving that sign of one of its already-sedimented layers of experience. It also projects the utopia of a pure and transparent, foundational sign: of a sign in charge of founding the positivity of a new order, free from opacities attesting to the negativity and heterogeneity of the social, which in turn make language and identity neither unified nor regular formations, but rather formations striated with conflict. The new feminist codification of the feminine cannot ignore the conflicted nature of signs (including "masculine" and "feminine") that operate as *axes of plurisignification*, intersecting various simultaneous and contradictory points of view about identity, power, and culture. Points of view deployed through hybrid formations, necessarily *impure* because they are traversed by signs belonging to uneven registers of clashing referents.

The same thing occurs with knowledge systems and theory. The fact that knowledge has a (masculine) master does not impede women from taking it over by storm and extorting those formulas that best prepare them to critique the masculinity of those knowledge systems. The fact that theory bears the registered trademark of masculine intellectualism—or that even in deconstructing it, we acknowledge that "the axioms of deconstruction frequently were put forth by men"[20]—does not bar us from stealing the toolboxes of a cultural theory legitimized and supervised by the masculine institutionalization of knowledge.

Julieta Kirkwood once said: "With respect to women, as with other marginalized categories, an expropriation of knowledge has been produced. Perhaps because of this, the ways of knowing recreated by women occasionally present an air of 'bricolage': concepts are taken from other paradigms and contexts, and invested with different meanings."[21] These operations of selection and combination, of resemanticization—to make enunciations speak *strategically*, rewriting or contradicting their points of origin when these dictate power—are operations common to all sub- and subaltern cultures. This "bricolage" of paradigms and discourses doubly identifies Latin American women. In their condition as female subjects and colonized speakers, they have always had to learn not only how to exploit to the fullest ways of reading between the lines of the colonial text restricting or prohibiting their "exercise of the word," but also to stitch together their own vocabularies with stolen (alien) meanings capable of subverting the colonialist dogma of the foundational text's purity and originality.[22]

These operations continue to be vital for any subcultural textual maneuvering that confronts the presumably foreclosed—finite —system of hegemonic categorizations symbolizing the authority of the Whole as metaphor for universal knowledge. To fragment or dislocate that system in order to reassemble its loose pieces in unknown combinations; to disorganize the coherent foci of meaning by multiplying discourse's lines of flight and dispersion; to upset the armature of enunciations so that peripheral citations can throw into crisis the imperialist model of unshakeable truths; to decenter the axes of official signification in order to liberate alternate and dissident routes for micropolitical readings: these are all operations of critical recontextualization that Latin American theory *knows* how to oppose to the mimetic guide of cultural transference offered by central and centrist models, including those of international feminism. Operations assuming that knowledge is not a system of laws guaranteed by the scientific orientation of their Method, but rather a field filled with tension by the never-resolved conflicts between the general and the particular, the totalizing and the fragmentary, the impartial and the partial, the serial and the discontinuous, the centered and the eccentric, and so on. The critique of knowledge which feminism can produce necessarily passes through this critical dismantling of forms of power and knowledge; it bases itself on the rules of the "tactical polyvalence" of discourses (Foucault) that enable a single enunciation to serve different ends depending on the type of critical recontextualization accommodating its signs in ways that are functional to each signifying operation. The same cultural discourse or enunciation of knowledge can, for this reason, articulate *different* politics of meaning and identity, because "discourse is not the site of pure subjectivity's eruption: it is a space of differentiated functions and subject positions."[23] The marks of the feminine and the masculine are *interactive conjugations* bringing these "differentiated functionings" into tension. More than resolve the problematic of difference seeking "an otherness in female lives and feminine ways of knowing" (the expression "another way of being")—or rather, more than rejecting as "not ours" (as "external") that which "does not emanate from us as women"[24]—feminist theoretical interventions must explode these games of differentiation from a conceptualization of gendered and sexual difference as a *transversal* axis for potentializing-activating and multiplying difference, so as to *pluralize* in these differences the "shared virtuality"[25] of the feminine.

TWO

Does Writing Have a Gender?

In August 1987, a group of Chilean women writers carried out an event, the first International Conference on Latin American Women's Literature,[1] which brought together multiple voices to address questions concerning the specificity and difference of "women's" writing.* All of these questions were contextualized within the conference by a double enunciatory mark: by the violence and political censorship of Chile under the dictatorship (within whose dislocated landscape the event took place) and by the marginality of Latin American culture with respect to metropolitan institutional and academic discourses. Although the first of these marks has been transformed by the democratic reopening, the second still remains in force, leaving us with the challenge of offering local reflections that must readjust the theoretical registers of imported knowledge (international feminist criticism) to the local demands and provocations of locally emergent poetics and narratives.

The results of that conference can be assessed, five years later, by taking into account several factors. A first positive effect seems to have been a coming to consciousness, more extensively shared by Chilean women writers, about the precariousness and ambiguity of inscription affecting "literature by women" within the frame of literary institutionality.[2] Another effect is the greater sociocultural exposure (and, consequently, increased access to publishing) around the theme of "literature by women" in Chile. It remains to be seen if the feminist theoretical formulations and articulations of that theme have been able to alter the assumptions and dispositions informing readings by established (academic, journalistic) critics and to instigate cultural debate in Chile's transition to democracy.[3]

In this essay, I will reexamine certain questions that the conference posed about the specificity and difference of "women's literature," dialoguing with some of the texts by those women (Raquel Olea, Eugenia Brito, Kemy Oyarzún, Adriana Valdés, Soledad Bianchi, Eliana Ortega, and others) who together have composed a space for feminist literary criticism in Chile today.[4]

It is now relatively agreed on that "in the last ten years in Chile, women have produced a notably high quantity and quality of literary texts."[5] Cited in support of this are the names of prose writers (Diamela Eltit, Mercedes Valdivieso, Ana María del Río, Pía Barros, Guadalupe Santa Cruz, Sonia Montecino, Agata Gligo, Marcela Serrano, etc.) and of poets (Carmen Berenguer, Soledad Fariña, Eugenia Brito, Teresa Adriasola, Malú Urriola, Nadia Prado, Marina Arrate, Carla Grandhi, Verónica Zondek, Teresa Calderón, Heddy Navarro, etc.)—a list bearing witness to a *collective* taking of the literary word by women.

In contrast to what has occurred traditionally, "only in the 1980s does the Chilean woman writer transcend her individual isolation. It would seem that for the first time one can speak of *women's writing* just that way, using the plural form."[6] And undoubtedly the 1987 Conference on Literature made visible—and public—the trajectory of that scene, which conformed and made manifest the *plural* quality of a constellation of voices marked by the same gender designation (being women). But is it the same to speak of "literature by women" as to speak of "feminine writing"?

Women's Literature and Feminine Writing:
How Is Gender-Sexual Difference Textualized?

"Literature by women" designates a set of literary works whose signature has a sexed valence, but that do not necessarily internalize the question of which constructions of language *textualize* gender-sexual difference. The category "literature by women" is used to delimit a corpus on the basis of a gender-sexual profile and to isolate that corpus in search of a relatively autonomous system of references-values conferring unity on the empirical sum of works it groups together. That is, "literature by women" sets up the sociocultural corpus that contains and sustains the question of whether characterizations of gender typifying a certain "feminine writing" exist.

Such characterizations can be traced at the *symbolic-expressive* level (the connotation of a feminine register whose style is particular to writing by women) or at the *thematic* level (a narrative argument centered on "images of women"). These "images of women" usually deploy a feminine structure of shared identification between the author and the character, as occurs when "a constant attempt to transgress the limits that separate the character from its creator exists. . . . The voice of the narrator, along with the character's, become one, with the intent to assume the feminine word in gendered terms. . . . The author not only invents but also becomes emotionally involved with her character."[7] Literary criticism that practices these expressive and thematic characterizations of the "feminine" is based on a representational conception of literature, according to which the text is called on to express realistically the experiential content of certain life situations, thereby portraying the "authenticity" of the female condition, or a certain "positiveness" in that the character exemplifies an antipatriarchal coming to consciousness. As Marcela Sabaj writes: "The story becomes a woman's body, is eroticized, self-destructs when abandoned, becomes stronger when set free, submits along with women in the condemnation of a sexist [*machista*] society. Every word attempts to construct the image of a self-sufficient woman."[8]

It seems to me that this type of criticism — by disregarding the signifying materiality of the writing complex (the signifying energy of the textual machinery) — is limited in several ways. On one hand, its naturalistic conception of the text, conceived as the expressive vehicle of experiential content, defines a realist and figurative treatment of literature. This conception fails in texts where writing itself is the protagonist of the work: deconstructing and reconstructing narrative codes, violating the stability of the referential universe, and disfiguring the presupposed verisimilitude of the mechanisms of feminine-literary personification and identification. On the other hand, this type of criticism makes the "feminine" a complete referent for an identity essence, able to be reuniversalized as such in its absolute genericness ("It is 'the woman' who speaks, she of all time, the same one as always, made to submit, tortured, suffering the disdain and oblivion of men").[9] And it fails to consider how identity and representation are made and unmade throughout the text under the demands of the linguistic-symbolic remodeling of writing. Both dimensions—writing as *textual productivity* and identity as the *play of representations*—should be incorporated by the new feminist literary theory to construct the "feminine" as the signified and *signifier* of the text.

But if we reject the thematic analysis of "images of women" as a method for defining the type of symbolic-literary correlations between *representations of gender* and *femininity* set up by the texts, we must ask ourselves once again: "What makes a written piece feminine writing? Is it possible for writing to be feminine? Is feminine writing a valid category? What feminine writing merits our attention as such? Do we have different expectations when we read poetic writing by a woman?"[10]

When the validity of the distinction between masculine and feminine textuality is questioned, many women writers, sensing the threat of seeing their rank lowered from the general (masculine-universal) to the particular (feminine), prefer to answer that there is only good or bad literature and that language does not have a gender. Adriana Méndez cites Cixous: "The majority of women that write have considered, until very recently, that they do so not as women, but rather as writers. Such women claim that their sexual difference doesn't mean anything, that there is no attributable difference between masculine and feminine writing."[11] Let us begin by revisiting Lyotard's words that "such a *neutralization* of the question [of the difference between masculine and feminine writing] is itself quite suspicious: just as when someone states that s/he is not political, is neither on the left nor the right, everyone understands that s/he is on the right."[12] That is, to say that language and writing are in/different to gender-sexual difference reinforces the established power by continuing to cover up the techniques through which a hegemonic masculinity disguises as neutral—as im/personal—its habit of personalizing the universal.

But to say that symbolic power maneuvers the marks of gender (as the ideological-sexual operators of a masculinization of culture), does not mean that writing itself (as signifying apparatus) obeys a monosexual key in its structure. Josefina Ludmer affirms that "feminine writing does not exist as a category because writing is asexual, bisexual, omnisexual."[13] I understand this affirmation best in relation to Julia Kristeva's theorizations,[14] agreeing that beyond the biological-sexual and psychosocial conditioning that defines the subject-author and influences certain modalities of cultural and public behavior, writing sets in motion an interdialectical crossing of various forces of subjectivity. At least two of them mutually respond to each other: the (feminine) semiotic-impulsive [*semiótico-pulsional*] force, which always overflows the finiteness of the word with its transverbal energy, and the (masculine) rationalizing-conceptualizing force, which symbolizes the institutionalization of the sign and preserves sociocommunicative limits. Both forces act together in every process of creative subject formation: it is the dominance of one force over the other that polarizes writing, whether in masculine terms (when the stabilizing norm is imposed) or in feminine terms (when a destructuring vertigo prevails). Certain cutting-edge experiences of writing venture toward those margins most explosive of dominant codes, as in the case of the literary avant-garde and neo-avant-garde. They unleash within language a heterogeneous impulse of the semiotic-feminine that explodes the sign and transgresses the paternal closure of monological significations, instead opening the word to a multiplicity of contradictory flows that give rhythm to syntactic rupturing.

Instead of feminine writing, it would be more apt to speak—regardless of the gender or sex of the biographical subject whose signature appears on the text—of a *feminization of writing*: a feminization produced each time a poetic or erotic sign exceeds the retaining/containing frame of masculine signification with its rebellious surpluses (body, libido, pleasure, heterogeneity, multiplicity, etc.) in order to deregulate the majority discourse's thesis. Any literature practiced as a *dissidence of identity* with respect to the normalizing format of the masculine-paternal culture, any writing making itself an accomplice of the transgressive rhythmicness of the feminine-impulsive, would deploy the minority and subversive (counterhegemonic) coefficient of the "feminine." Any writing in the position to undo the normalizing control of masculine/hegemonic discursivity would share the "becoming minority" (Deleuze-Guattari) of a feminine that operates as a paradigm of deterritorialization of the regimes of power and of captured identities, centered and regimented by the official culture. Diamela Eltit agrees with such a perspective:

> If the feminine is that which is oppressed by the central power, as much at the level of the real as on the symbolic planes, it is viable to recur to the materiality of that metaphor and amplify the category of gender in order to name as *feminine* all those groups whose position vis-à-vis what is dominant maintains the signs of a crisis. . . . It seems necessary to turn to the concept of naming as feminine that which from the margins of the central power seeks to produce a modification in the monolithic scheme of literary practice — regardless of whether its initiators are men or women — creatively generating meanings that transform the established symbolic universe.[15]

Identity and Disidentity:
The Pulse of Writing and Decentering the Subject

This theoretical aperture which extends the contestatory valence of the feminine to a range of antihegemonic practices—in order to weave solidarity-based alliances transversal to the categorizations of sex and gender linearly defined—holds, for me, the advantage of breaking down a biological determinism in which anatomical functions (being a woman/being a man) and symbolic roles (the feminine/the masculine) correspond naturalistically, based on the myth of an original body's Singular Identity. To uncouple both constructions from the naturalistic realism of the originating body permits the *signs* of the masculine and the feminine to become mobile, to become displaced and transformed according to the dynamics of subjectivity that each symbolic-sexual process progressively formulates in response to the call of the dominant social model of identity. Just as "being a woman" does not guarantee by nature the critical exercise of a femininity necessarily questioning of hegemonic masculinity (of its dominant cultural parameters), "being a man" does not condemn a subject-author to being fatally partisan to the official culture's codifications of power or to automatically reproducing its mechanisms, no matter how much organized patriarchy tries to convince him of its benefits. In fact, there are various convincing examples of practices by men (we should remember the authors of the poetic revolution analyzed by Kristeva) whose poetic and literary experimentation twisted language and identity to the point of completely decentering the ("phalogocentric") function-of-the-subject promoted by the dominant cultural ideology through its brokered codes.

If we resituate ourselves in the Chilean context of poetry under the dictatorship, the first poets to shatter the edifice of the "I" of epic and lyric traditions, and to cast its debris against the transcendental image of the metaphysical speaker, were Juan Luis Martínez, Raúl Zurita, Gonzalo Muñoz, Diego Maqueira, and others. Their practices carnivalized the "I" of history with transsexual parodies of masculine and feminine roles that alternated and rotated in the poet's voice montage, which was also the voice of the lumpen proletariat, the prostitute, the transvestite, the guerilla fighter, and the saint. Remembering those citations of the poetic-literary neo–avant-garde of the 1980s in order to *situate* the emergence of women's voices is a way of attending to Soledad Bianchi's request: "It becomes necessary to break the 'ghetto' of gender, which would involve situating them (texts by women) alongside those produced by their male and female contemporaries, considering their similarities and differences, recognizing achievements and contributions, but also their limitations."[16] By not recognizing those limitations, feminist criticism runs the risk of overprotecting the production of women and thereby prolonging its invalidity, marginalizing it from the battle-field of culture where signifying strategies struggle with each other. If "we indiscriminately shelter the artistic production of women based on the social irregularities that work against them as citizens,"[17] we might, in the name of Difference, censor an/other difference vital to feminist criticism. A difference that separates those feminine productions still subordinated to the dominant *forms* of cultural ideology (no matter how much feminist activism has questioned its thematic content) from those other feminist productions rebelling against the armatures of official culture and engendering techniques capable of unleashing conflicting readings in the interior of their socioliterary formalizations. This difference bears the same characteristic as that separating "two extreme tendencies in the cultural activity of the opposition. One tends to take for granted the processes of signification" and charges the ("already constituted") meanings with setting in motion the oppositional message. The other considers "the ideological character of the signification process . . . as itself something to be challenged," based on the idea "that dominant modes of representation constitute forms of subjectivity—the subject fixed by closure, for example—characteristic of a masculinist or patriarchal culture, and that to write 'in the feminine' is in itself to challenge the ideological constitution of the dominant modes of representation."[18]

To reincorporate writing by women into the intercrossing dynamics of historical sequences that give life to literary traditions is to pose the problem of the relationships between feminine texts and cultural intertextuality (predominantly masculine).

We know that the heritage of texts received as historical-cultural legacy was conformed according to the criteria for selection and interpretation of materials from the past fixing the (masculine) authority of historical knowledge in official culture. These criteria have progressively defined the Major Canon that every literature recognizes as a norm in order to deploy around it the dialectic of continuity and rupture articulating the relationship between texts and the codes for transmission of literary knowledge. The dynamism of this relationship depends on one's feeling an active part of tradition (even in order to break with it, in the style of a "heroic war against a precursor"[19] waged by the male writer), and not, as in the case of women, feeling excluded by it, or even led toward "servitude, discipleship, mimetism"[20] due to the weight of the official tradition's canonical authority when it is lived as alien and alienating.

But no literary tradition is hermetically sealed by the continuity of a single and unique voice: "It is worth wondering if, in effect, language is semiologically monopolized in its totality by the masculine point of view, or if, beyond institutional meanings, on the plane of linguistic norms, the possibility of change might not exist, as evidenced by the development of language, its history, and the arduous work of women themselves."[21] Language, history, and tradition are not unbreakable totalities but rather provisionary juxtapositions of multiple accounts that do not coincide, juxtapositions in which various historical meanings struggle against each other in battles between material and interpretive codes. Women cannot afford the luxury of not taking advantage of what is unleashed (of what is lost or gained) through these battles, since they all contain rebellions between the lines which can help to reinforce their own feminine enterprise of dismantling the symbolic-cultural edifice of patriarchal culture. Recovering those *decanonizing* voices (including the masculine ones) for women's benefit, and weaving antiofficial pacts with them, is as vital as deforming and resignifying the canon under the pressure of heterodox readings that subvert and pluralize the norm of literary knowledge. Adriana Valdés suggests just that,[22] following the line of analysis that Jean Franco has called "the struggle for interpretive power,"[23] with its respective strategies of resistance to normative dominant representations spoken from the *discursive position* of cultural subalternity.

Reframing the canon also implies modifying generic boundaries (in both senses of the word—of literary genres and sexual genders), shifting the masculine biases according to which official culture designs and reserves compartmentalized territories for each sex: domestic and familial interiority for women, social and political exteriority for men. Some feminine literary maneuvers seek to defeat those biases by reintentionalizing marks of the "feminine" (for example, intimism, biography, etc.) that have been discriminated against—as subjectivist expressions of the confinement of women in familial domesticity—investing them with a double *meaning* that enables them to parody and question that delimitation of space. But for that gesture to yield a critical effect, it not only must alter the literary content and forms thematizing the "private" in an obligatory feminine register; it also must deprivatize the gesture of reaccentuating the "private" (disassembling and mocking the politics of space in masculine/feminine ideology), so that it *problematizes* the scale of what is valued or not in a culture manufacturing the stereotypes of "privacy."[24] Without the polemical scope of that *transit* through the circuits of socioliterary ideology, the feminine remains in isolation, a reduction [*reducto y reducción*].

We know that many texts by women—because of passive imitation or filial subordination to the paternal authority of canonical tradition—merely obey the protocol of the dominant culture and reproduce its patterns of masculine subjugation. It is not sufficient, then, to be a woman (sexual determinant) for the text to be charged with the transgressive potential of minority writing. Women may take up the word only to pay a conformist tribute to the masculine assumptions of the established culture. Nor is it sufficient to deploy content based on the themes of women and feminine identity for the work with language to *produce* (and not simply reproduce) gendersexual differences encoded in the experiences of bodies and biographies.[25] So what characterizes or distinguishes a "women's" writing that seeks to textualize the feminine as active difference and *differentiation?*

Many women writers made the body—the register of the corporeal—into the focus of their response. The body as the first surface to be reconquered (to be decolonized) through a feminine autoeroticism of the letter and the page. An entire model of "feminine writing" based on the body's sexed correlate of identity/difference: the

morphological-sexual body of natural (originary) identity. An originary body always on the verge of reconfirming the Freudian decree
that "anatomy is destiny," when the texts do not sufficiently emphasize the mediating interventions of those cultural discourses charged
with turning the body into *writing*. In Soledad Fariña's words: "Re-
curring to the fiction of an originary place—lacking a meaning that
will collect the body's impulses—the terminal hand of a pulsing cur-
rent attempts to convert the writing act into a gesture. But does that
trace permit versions of syntax, of metaphorical structures, or of an
imaginary exposed in its difference to flourish?"[26]

How to specify, then, what is "particular" to the feminine without
remitting in an essentialist way to the metaphysics of being (in this
case, of "being a woman") as a natural referent of an identity *signed
by* and *consigned to* the fixity of an origin? And more radically: "What
can 'identity,' even 'sexual identity,' mean in a new theoretical and
scientific space where the very notion of identity is challenged?"[27]
The shattering of the subject and the decenterings of self that
contemporary theory radicalized through its antihumanistic slogan
of the "death of the subject" (at least, the death of the transcendental
self of metaphysical rationality) require that feminism rethink social and sexual identity. Identity not as a coherent self-expression of
a unified "I" (no matter how "feminine" a certain model might be),
but as a tension-filled dynamic crossed by a multiplicity of heterogeneous forces maintaining it in constant disequilibrium. How can
we still speak of *a* masculine identity or *a* feminine identity, as if they
were fixed and invariable terms instead of fluctuating constellations?
If feminism should have learned anything from psychoanalysis,
it is, first, that the subject of the sexual unconscious never coincides
with itself because masculine/feminine difference always traverses it
as the *internal contradiction* of a subjectivity in process and movement.
And second, that "femininity is not simply achieved and is never fully
reached."[28] And not because it is a pure void or deficiency, as the cas-
trating axiom of (Lacanian) Lack suggests, but because the relationship of women to meaning is never *total*, since its point of departure

is a basic inadequacy: one that makes her feel strange (and foreign) to the pact of social adhesion and cohesion that seals self-identity through its language of sociomasculine consensus, and in relation to which woman is always *less* (the feminine as symbolic deficit) or *more* (the feminine as impulsive excess).

That *misalignment* with relation to the borderlines of belonging and relevance [*pertenencia-pertinencia*] which map the configurations of social identity is not indifferent to the mode in which women experience themselves as a margin, shore, or border zone (placed at the outer limits) with respect to the system of cultural categories and symbolic systems. And while challenges to paternal authority are neither exclusive nor peculiar to women's practices, it is no less true that women face the alternative norm/infraction under special circumstances *especially* predisposing them to excess. Some women seek to conjure up the danger of crises capable of disintegrating social structures, exaggerating—defensively—their response of conformity to the ideologies of religious, familial, and national order.[29] Others disregard the symbolic-masculine mandate and launch their offensive against the patriarchal defense of the system of identity, unleashing in its interior the spasmodic revolt of disidentity. Writing is perhaps the place where that spasm of revolt operates most intensively: especially when the word, subjectivity, and representation disengage their ideological and cultural registers to the point of bursting the linguistic unity that ties meaning to the discursive economy of the phrase. And to the point of exploding with that unity the repressively oedipal-familial codes of identity, giving way to a transsexual rebirthing of a subject now "unmaternal and unpaternal" [*desmaterna y despaterna*], as occurs in Diamela Eltit's work,[30] clearly the most explosive in Latin American literature over these last few years.

THREE

Politics and Aesthetics of the Sign

Part of the debate surrounding women and artistic creation—alive in various international contexts—involves differentiating between a "feminine aesthetic" and a "feminist aesthetic." The definition of a "feminine aesthetic" usually connotes art that expresses woman as a natural (essential) fact and not as a symbolic-discursive category formed and deformed by systems of cultural representation. Feminine art would be any art representing a universal femininity or a feminine essence illustrating the universe of values and meanings (sensibility, corporeality, affectivity, etc.) traditionally reserved for women in the masculine-feminine binary system. It would be that art for which the feminine is the distinguishing and complementary characteristic alternating with the masculine, without questioning the philosophy of identity that regulates the unequal relationship between woman (nature) and man (culture, history, society) sanctioned by the dominant gender ideology. On the other hand, a "feminist aesthetic" would be that other aesthetic postulating woman as a sign immersed in a chain of patriarchal forms of oppression and repression which must be broken, through a coming to awareness of how masculine superiority is exercised and combated. Feminist art seeks to correct the stereotypical images of the feminine that the hegemonic masculine has gradually demeaned and penalized. An art motivated, in its form and content, by a critique of the dominant gender ideology. And more complexly, an art that intervenes in visual culture from the understanding of how codes of identity and power structure the representation of sexual difference to favor hegemonic masculinity.

Numerous exhibits organized in recent years in Chile to conse-crate the successful promotion of the subject of women—already domesticated as an international novelty by official cultural markets —are repositories of a conventional "feminine aesthetic." These mu-seum and gallery exhibits seek to emphasize the value and quality of women's art as a supposed reparation for their unjust historic relega-tion to a second tier of artistic and cultural figuration, but they lack any analytical framework or critical reflection. Above all, they lack a framework informed by feminist theory, which has taken on the task of problematizing:

1. The criteria for assigning aesthetic value to art. Jointly with the con-ditioning of race and class, gender operates as a marker of power influencing the scale of values that qualify or disqualify artworks de-pending on whether or not they respond to the hegemony of guide-lines fixed by the masculine discursivity of official culture.

    That judgment of "quality" seeks to make itself trustworthy (equitable) by pretending to rest on the neutral institutional recog-nition of women and men with works of equivalent merit. But how can we not doubt that judgment when we know that the formalist category of "quality" is not neutral (universal) but rather forged by a prejudicial culture that defends, among other interests, masculine supremacy as the absolute representative of the universal?

2. The measures for cataloguing works into series called "histories of art." Art history is a discursive formation whose paradigms for organizing knowledge (based on procedures involving the selection, evaluation, and classification of artworks) reflect a predominance of the type of historic rationalization that has conferred a masculine vector to social temporality.

    As Griselda Pollock states, "adding new materials—women and their history—to existing categories and methods"[1] does not alter the *systematicity* of the rationale traditionally responsible for marginalizing the feminine from its field of masculine self-referentiality. It is not merely a matter of women sharing equal conditions for facilitating their admission to the honorary framework of a universal art history, because it is that very "art history" that, as a *discursive series*, must be questioned in light of the suspicions raised by dominant-masculine historiography's tendentious archiving of the past.

Only through a debate capable of questioning the idealistic-bourgeois assumption of aesthetics as the pure and disinterested contemplation of beauty—a debate waged in the name of a critical materialist conception of art as a *practice of signs* inserted into the antagonistic and confrontational plots of the social—can the feminine exercise its transformative potential. That is, exercise its political-discursive power to disorganize cultural messages, those messages that totalize the masculine perspective as an *absolute* vantage point from which the revision and supervision of history and meaning take place.

Signs, Power, and Disobedience

It is interesting to recall two exhibits mounted outside of Chile during the military period in order to contrast them retrospectively with certain ones staged today. The two exhibits, realized in 1983 (*Chilenas* [Chilean woman], Berlin) and in 1987 (*Mujer, arte y periferia* [Women, art and periphery], Vancouver, British Columbia), managed to suggest at that time new and complex questions regarding the artistic gestures of Chilean women artists under the dictatorship.[2] Questions that wove together the theme of an artistic language based on the specificity-woman ("*identity*") posed by the gendered selection of the two shows, with the additional twist of a double *disidentification*: political exile in the case of Berlin, the Latin American periphery in the case of Vancouver. In both cases, situations of displacement—that drove these works on signs to be measured against the violence of place (Chile), but also that of no place (exile, periphery) —intervened in the feminine-feminist discussion about the "placement" of women's art. Both shows drove all questions regarding "identity-woman" to be formulated from the decentered geography of artworks crossed by errancy and transit. A geography that, metaphorically speaking, energized the feminist critique both of the sedentary "I" (the immobility of categories of sexual and social belonging) and of the invariability of meaning fixed by masculine decree.

These two shows incorporated as part of their selection the work of those visual artists who most actively participated in the artistic and critical reconceptualization of visual languages undertaken by the counterinstitutional practices of the so-called new scene [*nueva escena*][3] during the Chilean dictatorship. Practices for *unframing*, when *moving beyond the frame* (the breakdown of the pictorial monologue of the fine arts tradition), simultaneously transgressed—through their helter-skelter incursion into the social and political—the frameworks of meaning that militarism and patriarchy had placed under intramural vigilance. Catalina Parra, Diamela Eltit, Lotty Rosenfeld, and Virginia Errázuriz are some of the artists (with works included in the two exhibits mentioned above) who rearticulated the sociocritical function of art in a context of extreme repressive violence and ideological censorship.

What might one think of these works in relation to feminism's question regarding "woman's" difference in creative languages, regarding *how* that difference opposes the artistic and cultural system legitimated by the institutional consensus of the sociomasculine gaze? How do these works respond to feminism's theoretical question regarding the gestures and movements capable of making that *difference* ("woman") a critical *interference* perturbing the mechanisms of dominant visuality?

None of these artists made the subject of gender-sexual difference the explicit content of their work. Nor were the works discussed in the language of feminist theory for the simple reason that such theory did not yet hold critical currency in the Chilean artistic scene. Nonetheless, by deploying tactics of refutation and impugnment of the totalitarian-authoritarian matrix of official discourses, such works encouraged feminist readings attentive to the critical valorization of a "gendered practice": a practice exposing the cracks within the languages of symbolic and institutional power in order to build strategies of resistance against its dominant codes of signification and interpretation.

Catalina Parra was among the first Chilean women artists to test the limits of censorship under authoritarianism. In 1977 she exhibited *Imbunches** at the Epoca Gallery in Santiago, a body of work that camouflaged its social and political denunciation through the veils of a game of allusions-evasions, in which discourse and figure betrayed one another and in which both betrayed the journalistic news item.

Her work manipulated one of Chile's official icons (the newspaper *El Mercurio*) as a symbol of the distortions of meaning practiced under the media's communicative monopoly of a single obligatory truth that regimented the reading and interpretation of events. All the operations deployed by Parra's work vis-à-vis the imposition-imposture of the truth dictated by the official press were intended to open gaps (cracks, fissures) in the interior of the fraudulent construction of coercive messages, so as to damage their consistency and strength. Parra's work metaphorized the act of violating the official press's slogans as an act of *wounding meaning* through a whole repertoire of surgical interventions and materials (gauze, bandages, stitches, etc.). This act made the scar an ambivalent mark: a mark resulting from a homicidal cut (slashing through lies), but whose lesion needed to be wrapped artisanally in a reparatory manual gesture, one that grafted and transplanted, that meticulously reconstituted delicate plots of antirepressive meanings, to render less intimidating those readings enforced by the "culture of fear." The scar was, then, the published reenactment of "the hidden war between words and images," playing with the notion that the word is *masculine* (the paternal antecedent of symbolic-cultural verbalization, in its theoretical history and biographical memory)[4] and that the image is *feminine* (because of its struggle against the overdetermination of univocal speech). Catalina Parra's work fractured the (typo) graphic body type of the press communiqué, constructing interpretive litigations around the truths that the all-powerful official message decreed inexpugnable. A fracture created in order to communicate to us that there is no register of words whose legibility, programmed from the position of authority, cannot be deprogrammed (unauthorized) by ruptures in signification that cut or loosen the links between power and its enunciative rituals.

A few years later, another woman's performance (*Una milla de cruces sobre el pavimento* [A mile of crosses on the pavement], Lotty Rosenfeld, 1980) turned to a new gendered mark to configure signs, power, and disobedience.[5] Speaking literally, the gendered mark was a white cloth bandage used to cross traffic lines, transforming the minus (–) sign into a plus (+) sign along the length of several Chilean and international avenues and freeways. But it was also an image of the feminine derived from the textile art of crossing threads: that is to say, the metaphor of a women's practice that unweaves the warp and plot of social communication, crossing along the way what has been tacitly negotiated through signs of masculine exchange.

Rosenfeld's work with crosses contains several highly significant dimensions for a feminist gaze interested in dismantling the (masculine) rules overseeing the linguistic transmission of social content. But these dimensions are constructed from a very first gesture: the deidealization of art as transcendence, as immaterial. A gesture constructed when the artist bends down over the city's pavement in order to make visible the materiality of the design composing the figures of social regulation (in this case, the physical texture of the marks that call to order by regulating traffic) and when she exhibits the decomposing of that mechanism, making graphic the antidisciplinary impulse hidden in the recesses of daily life. By converting the minus (–) sign into a plus (+) sign, crossing with her body the marks that signal the flow to follow as the routinary disciplinary model for centuries, Rosenfeld commits an infraction against the unidirectionality —the one-way traffic—of meaning. She obstructs the forced march forward, deviates from the flow that leads to what a teleological horizon categorically programs as the goal. In the context of a country where signs are guarded by the inviolability of coordinates sheltering the fixity of order, she twists the coherence and legibility of a part of the social order (traffic lines) in order to demonstrate that all of power's sign systems are susceptible to being disobeyed, bit by bit, until, extensively, the grammar of order itself finds its own organizing principle (the immutability of signs) threatened.

Rosenfeld marked with a cross those sites that offered a particular symbolic concentration of authority on the map of sociomasculine exchanges of political and economic power (Washington, D.C., and the Santiago Stock Exchange, respectively). But the cross also served to make political rationales, social misery, and critical utopias intersect, as when Rosenfeld concluded a phase of her work in the unfinished San Miguel Hospital (December 1989). The new cross on the screens of this video installation was formed with the vertical and horizontal lines marking a vote in the 1988 plebiscite, as an image of democracy to come. That new mark of the cross signaled the pluriideological crossroads of a history inverting the arithmetic of the power of signs and the signs of power, converting the minus (the sign that subtracts and divides: the dictatorship) into a plus (the sign that *multiplies*: democratic plurality). From sign to sign, this work, itself always crossed by a woman's gesture, proved transversal to the process of historical erasure of Manichaean divisions of meaning (the concentrating stripe of the dictatorship), joining the desire to render the codes of cultural intervention multidimensional in a democratic weave graphed through the addition and multiplication of difference.

Virginia Errázuriz's work also reflects on marks, directions, and orientations—on the groupings of signals that guide our perception of space in the service of a surveying functionality. Errázuriz also proposes that we self-critically unlearn the scripts leading to the passive and imitative consumption of the signs that transmit information. Only she does so not by engaging social exteriority but rather by employing the interior of art spaces (galleries, museums) to support her artistic *destructuring* of space. Her work consists of the fractioning-out of visual groupings that defy the reunifying syntheses of a general point of view: the point of view that summarizes and concludes. It decenters that point of view, invalidating its power to account for wholeness and totalities, conceding to it only fragments and remains of geometries lost in those zones lowest in the room's hierarchy (for example, corners). That dehierarchization of the gaze, lowered to the (non-) height of the floor or marginalized toward lateral locations, seeks to complicate—to impede—the exercise of dominant visuality: to deviate it toward the least stable surfaces, where the syntax of seeing is interrupted by breaks in perspective shattering the control of a superior vision, supported by the certainty of a frontal master gaze.

These discontinuities of the visual field correlate significantly with the narrative disarticulations of a reading made hollow by voids of signification: blank spaces—or spacings—that suspend and defer the task of completing meaning. The work de-emphasizes the referential weight of signs through a precarious object emphasis on the minimal and intimate, signaling the *detail* as an antideclamatory recourse to be contrasted with heroic-masculine phraseology. Against the grandiloquent rhetoric of monumental history, Errázuriz always worked with halting significations, diminutive fictions made of fragile lexicons, which displaced attention toward zones less saturated with explanatory verbalism. As if only the *intermittencies of meaning* were able to modulate the failure of totalizing metanarratives exhausting planes and surfaces through their summary overaccumulation of rationales and readings without loose ends.

The three artists mentioned formulated a critique of official mechanisms of signification through the image (Parra), the gesture (Rosenfeld), and the gaze (Errázuriz). Diamela Eltit participated in that critique with flights of words that wandered and digressed outside literary institutions.

In the years preceding and accompanying the publication of her first novel (*Lumpérica*, 1983), she performed acts of urban intervention which took beyond the text (the book format) those textual excesses that the novel documented as art and refictionalized as literature. These street actions marked a first contact between bits of writing as they were being produced (as *Lumpérica* was being written) and their public reading taped on film and video in a brothel on Maipú Street (1980).† The brothel was also the trysting place [*la casa de citas*] where techniques and genres came together illicitly (performance art, video, film, literature) to vie for the favor of a transitory word. In the midst of a poor neighborhood street, the aim was, among other things, that literature's gratuitous (sumptuous) word—parading the luxury of its baroque verbosity in the face of the poverty of prostitution—break down an economy of sexual commerce and debunk the assumption of masculine profit through the exchange of money, words, and women. As when she kissed the vagrant in the video *Trabajo de amor con los asilados de la hospedería* [Labor of love among the dwellers of a Santiago boardinghouse] (1982), Eltit released into free circulation the pleasure of a word offering itself up for nothing: just to do so/for art/for the love of art. With this *wasting*, she shattered the transactional market of goods and services destined exclusively for masculine retribution.[6]

The video documentation of Eltit's work not only registered its break by failing the socially valued model of art and culture; it also modeled that *failure* as a minority aesthetic. Only the "bad image"[7] —in contrast to the technical hypercontrol of a gaze expert in the visuality of consumption—was capable of reaestheticizing imperfections and blunders in symbolic homage to the failings of narrations seemingly transparent and too sure of themselves. The "bad image" was a Third World metaphor for technological failure, for the imperfections spoiling the self-approved visuality of the metropolis, creating critical interferences on its screens through the opacity of the residue, the discard. But the "bad image" was also the feminine *errata*, an error worked on as such, against the model of perfection victoriously raised by a masculine gaze thought to be "beyond suspicion." It was this tremor of the inexact that made the pseudocertainty of the master image vacillate.

These feminine thematizations of the "bad image" were part of what video art (mostly practiced by women) proposed, generating polemics at a time when video festivals were the obligatory tribunals of Chilean artistic and critical debate regarding the politics of the audiovisual sign.[8] A debate that challenged—using the neo-experimental profile of the "problem works" authored by women—the "theorem-thought" of those who defended the specificity of the medium in the name of a theoretically oriented formalism, isolating the supposed purity of the video signifier from all interaction with social or sexual contexts.

A look at the video program organized as part of the 1991 exhibit *Mujeres en el arte* [Women in art][9]—in which the names of Lotty Rosenfeld, Gloria Camiruaga, Tatiana Gaviola, Macarena Infante, Jessica Ulloa, Patricia Mora, and Angela Riesco, among others, appear or reappear—should suffice for conveying the continued meaningful participation of women in this field. Gone from the scene, however, are the aforementioned discussions regarding the "emancipatory postulate" of "Video-Feminism," with its "constant search for structures and treatments that, in the case of video art, could be differentiated from those entrenched in the system" of dominant audiovisuality.[10] The problematic of video—whether as an alternative format for communication linked to social action projects mobilized by the opposition under the dictatorship (video *testimonio*), or whether as an expressive support for formal experimentation (fiction and art video) developed by filmmakers or visual artists—has been recycled by the normalization of spaces for sociocultural participation under democratic institutionality.

One of the spaces that generated expectations of a redefined democratic sensibility was television. In this context, some dreamed it appropriate to ask: "Through what politics can the aesthetic and ideological innovation [of video art] reenter into communication" with the tendencies "of the most influential medium in contemporary society?"[11] Chilean television rapidly made abundantly clear, however, that it had eliminated from its screens all critical-aesthetic proposals that unsettled the rules of visual consumption dictated by the market's homogenizing rhetoric. This rhetoric not only obstructs the possibility of expressing the heterogeneity of social forces and cultural energies coexisting unevenly in society.[12] It also entails the critical disempowering of those investigations that tend to relate the dynamics of constituting the identities of new social actors (women, for example) with the creation of new languages and cultural forms that do not confuse their signs with those of the dominant aesthetic. Up to now, the insertion of women into Chilean television has been relegated to programs that highlight female performances (the "political woman," the "business woman," etc.) resulting from the advances of social democratization, without allowing the portrayal of these new forms of protagonism to alter the laws of gender typifying the content and *styles* of the "feminine" repeated in the social sphere. The traits that frequently individuate feminine journalism on television are the spontaneity of conversational exchange and biographical intimacy. Traits that supposedly express woman's greater receptivity to the "human" (understood as the *private nature* of emotions and feelings), as if the value of that affective disposition were not already calculated by the masculinist distribution adjudicating to man the value of abstraction (transcendence) and to woman the value of concretion (immanence). A distribution intended to dissuade women from daring to take part in the *politics of meaning*.

Art-System and Aesthetic Critique

The interest shown by Chilean women artists in manipulating video images was formalized during the period of most lively discussion regarding the critical potential of the languages of aesthetic tradition (a potential marked by the fragmentation of referents and symbols during the 1973 military takeover). Such discussions took place under circumstances in which these languages seemed to have exhausted their ability to reinvent signs that could account for the historic fracturing of memories and identities without surrendering to the disintegrative violence of the crisis.

Despite the vast and staggering historical and political differences separating the two contexts, Chilean women artists' choice of "anticlassical" languages coincides with an international tendency characterizing feminist art in England and the United States in the seventies and eighties (at least in the practices of artists like Mary

Kelly, Barbara Kruger, Sherrie Levine, Cindy Sherman, Jenny Holzer, etc.).[13] First, their work is *anticlassical*: it makes explicit their distrust of the patriarchal propensity for the mythology of art incarnated by the academicist cult of a master tradition. It does so by using materials and techniques alien to that tradition's repertoire and connected instead to mass visuality (the television image, the press photo, the ad campaign, etc.), so as to deconstruct its codes using the very materiality of the signs that make it the bearer of social stereotypes. Relocated in the international artistic context of the seventies and eighties, however, the photographic visuality of those international feminist practices also sought to respond to the market's repositioning of the pictorial trans–avant-garde and the depoliticization of art promoted by the critique of neo–avant-garde experimentalism and dictated by the "postmodernism of reaction."[14] The Chilean works mentioned here knew how to link the "difference" of their practice as women with the "alternative" search for methods of intervening in the art system, so as to bring into conflict the contemplative ritualism of the painting and to mobilize their counterinstitutional proposals beyond the museum's foreclosing frame.

There is another similarity between the production of Chilean women artists and North American feminist art of the eighties: their "alliance with theory" and their "regard [for] critical or theoretical writing as an important arena of strategic intervention."[15] All the artistic reformulations practiced by the Chilean women were accompanied by texts dedicated to the theoretical reconceptualization of artistic and cultural thought under the dictatorship—texts that proposed a critical interaction between theory and practice as part of an effort to construct an active dialogue with the social and political reflections of those years.[16] Both circumstances changed.

The democratic transition's political reformulations modified the arena of artistic and cultural practice. The bipolar dynamic of frontal confrontation between the official and nonofficial, which rigidly overdetermined the art of the dictatorship, was broken. The severe topography of exclusions, relegating what was prohibited to a decisive "outside" of the system, became obsolete. Institutional-democratic consensus today drives the integrated and the rejected to combine their margins with fluidity and ambiguity *within* the same system, thanks to an ingratiating pluralism. When the violent antagonism connoted by a politics traversed only by the hard logic of confrontation became dedramatized, cultural practices had to redesign their imaginary of rupture, previously linked to a purely oppositional art that extracted its *pathos* from confrontational negativity. These practices also had to rearticulate their operational dynamics in terms more suited to the multidirectionality of social forces and communicative tensions under democracy. Moments of perplexity and disorientation followed the shift in rules that caused the relationship between art and politics to become depolarized. And to become defused and often relaxed within the pragmatics of bureaucratic-administrative accommodations inviting artists today to renounce critical radicalism in order to dedicate themselves to negotiating maneuvers. This new political-institutional adjustment normalized the functioning of cultural circuits, returning to each practice its regular space of inscription, recuperating through them the specificity that corresponded to each before the dictatorship drove culture to cross over as a substitute political platform, at the time placed under the interdiction of word and action. In the case of art, practices were reintegrated into the Museum and galleries. Art's force of interpellation in the eighties, which brought together a multiple and mixed (literature, philosophy, social sciences) public around polemics "beyond the frame," was neutralized with the reframing of the arts in a network of exhibits and markets separated and disengaged from any real power of cultural interlocution.

Women's practices and reflection about them also lost intensity due to the lack of a theoretically informed artistic debate. Which is not to say that Chilean art has no talented painters (Gracia Barrios, Roser Bru, Patricia Israel, etc.) or new proposals deserving of critical attention (Nury González, Alicia Villareal, etc.). Only that, in contrast to literature, these works do not intersect with readings that analyze them from the perspective of their gendered markings. Such a perspective would open with questions about the relationship between *feminine authorship* (being a woman) and *feminism* (signifying organization and cultural intervention) in the sense of asking what the mechanisms of critical dismantling might be which allow one to subvert the masculine organization of social registers for manufacturing meaning. In the absence of such a perspective, the opportunity dissipates for the woman question to detonate a polemic reflection in art—for example, the modes in which a "feminine aesthetic" and a "feminist aesthetic" respond contradictorily to the relationship between gender-sexual determinants and the notions of "femininity" that the work seeks to construct or deconstruct. A reflection beginning with the understanding that "the questions of identification, self-definition, the modes or the very possibility of envisaging oneself as subject—which the male avant-garde artists and theorists have also been asking, on their part, for almost one hundred years, even as they work to subvert the dominant representations or to challenge their hegemony—are fundamental questions for feminism."[17] This "envisaging oneself as subject" does not mean self-contemplation as "woman" in the image of a complete femininity. It means, rather, to render operative those constructions of the subject that can be deployed between codes, seeking in each interstice of discourse the opportunity to create a strategic response to the institutional categories of identity and representation derived from the "feminine," as the position-articulation of an alternative and dissident subjectivity.

FOUR

Gender Contortions and Sexual Doubling:

Transvestite Parody

Artistic imagery invoking the figure of the transvestite* (art, photography, video, literature, theater) exploded under the dictatorship, in a Chile that joined in a single image two counterposed signals of gender: *active* (domination) and *passive* (submission). On one side of this double face, the Chile involved in taking power and in armed intervention imposed a militaristic-patriarchal discourse, exacerbating the ruling rhetoric's virile identifications. And on the other side of this very same face was the Chile submerged in obedience to the disciplinary model, submitting to orders, like a woman, in obligatory silence.

During these years of clandestine and repressed desires, the figure of the Chilean transvestite, which emerged from within the most tortuous shadows of the codes for regimenting meaning, unearthed this double ordering of masculinity and femininity, at once deeply regulatory and merely superficial. The convulsion of the transvestite's asymmetrical madness burst into a wry expression of identity which signaled the failings of uniform(ed) and uniforming genders, dissolving their faces and facades into a doubly gendered caricature that shattered the mold of dichotomous appearances, a mold fixed by rigid systems of national and civil cataloguing and identification.

The visual arts were the first space to introduce the theme of a gay aesthetic as a form of questioning sexual identity and social repression, patriarchal culture and liberating utopias of revolutionary desire.† The performances of Carlos Leppe during the 1980s and Juan Dávila's artistic work constitute two decisive precedents in this regard.[1]

Both artists' work incorporated discourses *of* and *about* the sexual unconscious into a play of citations: restaging their figures (the narcissistic wound of castration in Leppe's work, retouched by his mother's biographical narration on video) or casting irony on the theses of psychoanalytic knowledge (Dávila) through counterillustrations borrowing from the comic strip its lack of depth in order to mock the dogma of occult and secret interior meanings with which psychoanalysis cultivates its following. Both bodies of work inverted and subverted the classical relationship between art and psychoanalysis, in that it was no longer psychoanalytic theory that interpreted the work of art (the work as symptom, as a representation of psychosexual content), but rather artistic discourse that revised and critiqued the reductionism of psychoanalytic readings of art conceived as the *reformed formation* of a conflict and not as a *deforming form*: as the transformative dynamic for articulating signs whose working force resymbolized the tension between energy and meaning.

It was these works that introduced the theme of psychoanalysis into Chilean art through the question of homosexual desire. A question to which one lone text valiantly did justice: Patricio Marchant's,[2] written apropos of a performance video completed by Leppe and Dávila in 1982.[3]

Marchant spoke of that inaugural presentation in Chile: "Its . . . concept . . . refer[red] to the production of a *happening*, not to a chronological relation" in which "the gay work of art, its scene, had to be presented, had to face, *others*," by staging "the general situation of the Latin American body, and the particular situation of Latin American homosexual desire."[4] This was set forth for the first time in that "inaugural" text, posed from the contortions of power-desire-knowledge, as a situation of

1. fracture and fracturing of the dominant culture's official discourse, starting from a fugitive subjectivity. Marchant explains: "Because by its marginality and exteriority, the gay movement is in an advantageous position to see the cracks, the falseness in official discourse, to see how official discourse finds itself obliged to invent certain Transcendental Signifieds which may serve to plug up a discourse leaking on all sides";[5]

2. lapsing into the temptation of the apocalyptic truth of the Transcendental Signifier by raising the vindicating banner of a new identity-Reference.[6] Marchant continues: "But once faced by the spectacle of these cracks, this falseness, the gay movement rushes in to fill the vacuum, declaring . . . that official discourse has been shattered because it has failed to recognize the homosexual nature of the truth, the homosexual nature of art," thus expressing "the need to hold in discourse with a homosexual plug";[7]

3. knowing that the theology of naming is a mockery to be deconstructed, in spite of the temptation to reinscribe the contestatory gesture into another emblem of identity. In Marchant's words, "the gay work of art is compelled to have recourse to ultimate Signifiers, 'sensational,' monotheistic, . . . at the same time [that it] *cannot but be aware* of the farcicality of the movement which results in creating such signifiers."[8]

The antipatriarchal knowledge that "names do not have single true meanings" — the antimetaphysical knowledge that only a fluctuating meaning revokes the closure of absolute truth — encountered its most transgressive expression in the parodic parade of names that Leppe's and Dávila's works engaged as a *transvestite metaphor*. Using the format of performance or painting,[9] both bodies of work began by questioning the myth of individuality-originality consecrated by the ideology of the *signature* in the bourgeois art tradition, revealing what the author's name symbolized by carrying out operations that demythologized the patriarchal canon of authorship-authority.

Both artists also took exaggerated recourse to citations and inter-citations, postulating the artwork as a zone of exchange, appropria-tion, and counterappropriation of dispersed enunciations selected from the international artistic repertoire and crossing each other through various regimes of *borrowing and lending* but also of *misappro-priating* techniques and styles. This recourse deindividualized the re-served space of the signature, shifting to the institutional symbolism of the painting the knowledge that a "name in which nothing is in-cluded" (Marchant), or a name in which all are included, is a name forever dysfunctional for the patrimonial regimes that legalize the Subject as the only owner of a Singular identity.

Along with that recourse, which laughs at the notion of autho-rial credit by discrediting the value of the work's originality as the stamp of property guaranteed by a name, Leppe and Dávila added the strategy of retouching their biographical names (Leppe—La Muñeca del Continente [the doll of the continent] or María Dávila) in their works, creating a transvestite spectacle through a poetics of nick-naming. Both transferred to art the transvestism of naming and the transvestite's decorative impulse, which refashions the name as a first matrix of identity in order to correct the defect of monosemia through and with added elements. This constitutes the first cere-mony of a refounding of identity, in which the transvestite consum-mates the act of disaffiliation, betraying the definitive quality of in-herited names (one's proper name) with transitory names—Marilyn, Sultana, Brigitte, and so on—that rebaptize, but without the onto-logical weight of the birth date's designated saint, now profaned by the exuberance of a capricious pseudonym.

In all of his latest work, Dávila reinforces the metaphor of trans-vestism by painting the transvestite as a parody of the parody of a parody: Latin America. The hyperallegorization of *identity as a mask* that transvestites in makeup achieve, unmasks the Latin American vocation of *retouching* [retoque]. Retouching the lack of what is "our own" (due to the deficit of originality that marks secondary cul-tures as cultures of reproduction) through the cosmetic—alienat-ing—overmarking of disguising oneself with what is "another's."

Viewed from the center, the peripheral copy is a diminished double, a devalorized imitation of an original that enjoys the added value of being a metropolitan reference. But viewed from itself, that copy is also a postcolonial satire of how First World fetishism projects onto the image of Latin America false representations of originality and authenticity (the primitivist nostalgia of the virgin continent), which Latin America again falsifies into a caricature of itself as Other to satisfy the other's demands. It is the mocking overacting of Dávila's transvestite in makeup—the plagiarized rites of a truncated femininity and of poor taste—that denounces the bazaar-based exoticism fueling the sale of Latin American trinkets in the market of postindustrial icons. And it is that same feminizing overacting of *posing as what one is not* (neither feminine nor original) that also resignifies the copy—and its mechanisms of doubling and simulation—as a critique from the periphery of the (paternal) Eurocentric dogma of the sacredness of the foundational model, unique and true, of metropolitan signification.

The transvestite fantasy of posing as what one is not conjugates in the apparatus of the gaze the knowledge that "ambiguously, desire is achieved, and simultaneously, in a provisional way, it is frustrated," given that "cosmetics and fashion are passing alterations, just as fleeting and transitory as the transformation achieved by a man who wants to and, if only for a brief instant, can be a woman."[10] The web of attraction and seduction in which the narcissistic impulse to appear as a transvestite gets tangled is necessarily optical, since it is the gaze of the other that determines the success or failure of the visual trap of passing *effectively* as a woman. The photographic image fixes (detains and retains) the instant in which the metamorphosis becomes complete as a cosmetic achievement for the gaze, not yet ruined by the physical suspicion of deceit. The photograph that captures the image of deceit in order to make it last over time and thereby ward off the frustration of disillusionment, grants a new supplement of durability to the already *supplementary* (accessory) femininity of transvestites, rewarding their vanity with a substitute image that delays the lapsing of concealment and prolongs the usurping of identities. Paz Errázuriz's photographed series of transvestites[11] time and again plays with the transvestite's fascination with everything that reproduces the image of sexual duplication (mirrors, the camera), thus multiplying delight in the conversion through a specular vertigo. The photos make the labyrinth of the transvestite's pose in the mirror reverberate. But breaks in perspective sidetrack the spectator's gaze toward nonfrontal aspects of the self-portrait: toward lapses in the nonpose that confess the asymmetry between obverses (a laboriously constructed allegorical femininity) and reverses (the literally masculine, surprised and betrayed by the undoing of what was until then its best angle). Lapses that foreshadow the terror that the transvestite subterfuge be discovered, threatening the panic-filled revelation of a woman with a penis: the woman who conserves underneath her disguise the attribute of virility, the man/woman associated, in a psychoanalytic register, with the traumatic motif of the phallic mother.

But Errázuriz's portraits of transvestite prostitutes play with obverses and reverses in other senses as well. Moving beyond the ambiguities of bodily seduction leads one to "encounter the other image, that of the signs of social abandonment those bodies construct" as a "stage traversed with the cracks"[12] of Chilean shantytown poverty.

It is shantytown poverty that organizes the backdrop of deprivations on which the exhibitionistic squandering of their passion for makeup is laid out with maximally contrasting hues. That conjugation of the prostitute and the transvestite, at once Chilean and of the shantytowns, dramatizes two economies, or rather, one economy and its antieconomy. While sexual commerce guarantees daily survival through the prostitute's body, a body *for sale* by obligation (sex-necessity), the transvestite's body *lends itself* to the cosmetic expending of a sex fantasy that cashes in realism for illusion, overturning the daytime law of indigence with the illegalisms of an opulent and sumptuous femininity hyperbolized at night (being a star) through the resplendent arabesques of the divine diva.

The "contiguous relationship between *sexual* marginalities (that attack the order of sexual reproduction) and *economic* marginalities (that attack the order of social production)"[13] has its map of encounters and frictions in the city.

In a 1982 interview conducted by the poet Raúl Zurita, Ernesto Muñoz (another artist positioned as gay) was already paying a streetwalker's tribute to the vagaries of desire:

> A gay trajectory breaks down the prison walls of neighborhoods, and on breaking them down, passes through and penetrates all social classes. The city has a rigid social organization that gays rupture, because they can be with a banker, and then two hours later with a worker or lumpen in some other sector of the city, with an equal sense of belonging in both places. That is the tremendously transgressive quality of gay movement: it breaks down the reality of class through the mapping of desire.[14]

The nomadic pulsation of gay desire—that inverts hierarchies of urban behavior, altering diagrams and programmed routines with the sexual whims of fantasies adrift[15]—provides both the pulse and impulse for place-specific eroticisms to flow out through sub-urban escape routes. Las Yeguas del Apocalipsis [The Mares of the Apocalypse], a gay Chilean art collective formed in 1987 by Pedro Lemebel and Francisco Casas, place *sexual errancy* and *artistic vagrancy* into a correlation of transits. Erratic presentations—meandering through the modes of performance, fashion show, miming, parody, farce, tableau vivant, ragtag circus, and happenings—stage transvestism as urban entertainment, "relegating the institution of art to the burlesque frivolity of commercial cinematography."[16] This burlesque frivolity plays itself out also, and above all, in the gesture of confusing the limit that separates and opposes the system of *work* (with its morality of effort) to the recreational interlude of *parties* as antisystem. Hence Las Yeguas' presentations shift the borders drawn by a legislation of daily life discriminating between utility (placed in the service of accounting for productive return) and its opposite (the pleasure of diversion).

The transvestite's parade through the portrait gallery of trafficked poses (the masquerade of "femininity as a masquerade")—performed by Las Yeguas when they imagine themselves as the last Hollywood appearance of a glamorous diva in decline—restylizes a convention of the feminine, now riddled with overmarkings. Transvestites need to disguise the woman (cover her image with signs, mask her with figures) in order to dress up like her by stealing her masks. Transvestites are officiants of an always ceremonial femininity, revering in a profane cult to *effigies* of the feminine. From there stems their passion for films that deify women through the auratic image of the movie star. Transvestite rites of sexual conversion, involving *representations* rather than substance, require taking women's roles from them (that is, everything that ties them to a servitude of tasks) in order to take possession of their images and appearances. Transvestites privilege the irrealism of *effect* (which glitters in the showiness of artifice) over the realism of *function* (dulled by routines and obligations).

From "the grotesque ugliness of its transvestite imitators," the whole hyperrhetorical quality of the feminine springs into view, thanks to their counterfeiting acts: the assembly of a facade offering an iconographic cult to Beauty, the stereotyping of the model in mimetic fabrication of women's roles. Transvestites make all this unravel when they explode the correspondence of sex and gender through their own anatomical incongruence.

In the previously mentioned interview, Ernesto Muñoz explains why the simulacrum of sexual conversion is punished as a mockery by the "stronger" sex's moral standards, which rely on a strict *rigor of truth* (an explanation he discards with regard to his own practice). Muñoz states: "Transvestites are homosexuals who cover and escape from themselves. They are no longer Pedro or Juan, but Roxana. With transvestites, truth looms large, but falsehood looms even larger. When you work with transvestites in art, you are not offering correct information. This creates difficulties for the spectator."¹⁷ Difficulties that, beyond sexual titillation, have to do with the concealment of truth: with privileging the falsehood of appearances over the truth of essences, with letting oneself be mesmerized by the brilliance of the artificial, with taking off and putting on masks and disguises to make the transcendental continuity of *being* vacillate (in an antifoundational way) through the alternation of *appearances*.

To make oneself doubly gendered through disguises that parody the merely ornamental clause of femininity in order to simulate-dissimulate solely through strategies of appearance, to remit human expression and its phraseology of sincerity to a dramatics of poses retheatricalized by makeup—these are acts that could only disappoint and ridicule the patriarchal faith in theologies of meaning upholding interior truths, the sincere expression of an authentic and profound "I." Insubstantial and desubstantiating, transvestism could only find itself censored by political dogmas promoting the *thesis* (truth) of social change, even when it was the thesis of gay liberation undergirding homosexual activism that was being promoted. When Pedro Lemebel describes the November 1991 Primer Encuentro de Homosexuales [First Meeting of Homosexuals] in Concepción, Chile, he speaks of how

> ideological diversity, a product of political orphanhood, progressively dismantled the linear scheme that the group MOVILH (Movimiento de Liberación Homosexual [Chilean Movement for Homosexual Liberation]) had developed as its strategy, with the unpleasant aftertaste of old party-based articulations. Such articulations progressively emerged through the acid parodies of Las Yeguas del Apocalipsis, parodies carried out with the complicity of lesbians and *locas* [drag queens or madwomen], offering an antidiscourse that made the serious homosexuals of the capital shake with anger.¹⁸

The transvestites' "acid parody" deceives the phallocratic discourse of Homo (homosexual/homological) self-representation by playing with couplings and uncouplings of meaning in a theater of uncertainty that is also a comedy of substitutions, starting with sexual marks that are as ambivalent as they are hypothetical. While homosexual discourse reproduces the erect logic of regulatory meanings in the hard line of the Revolution of desire, transvestite discourse aestheticizes and feminizes itself: it copies the tricks of the "weaker" sex in order to weaken revolutionary ideologism, playing the *loca* with her pseudosemantics of transverse genders. Before those programs of homosexual vindication, as well as feminist ones (in the case of an essentialist feminism that renders the subject-woman absolute as its complete and total referent), it could be that the "peripheral persona" of the transvestite, with her roaming metaphor of superimposed and interchangeable identities, presents "one of the most potentially subversive challenges" confronting systems of univocal categorization of normative identity. This is due to how transvestites "sacrifice foundational equality for transformational difference. By ignoring the traditional hierarchy between appearance and essence, interior and exterior, reality and simulation . . . they acquire an unknown mobility, free at last of artificial restrictions (biological and social consistency, geographic delineations, historical compulsions) imposed on them by the dominant culture in the name of essential purity."[19]

But this description of the transvestite by Celeste Olalquiaga corresponds to the gay Latino in New York—a postmodern metaphor of the recycling of identities that mixes definitions of First World and Third World, ransacking the metropolis's shop windows and repertoires of signs. Latin American transvestites stage a different simulacrum through their *neobarroco* [neobaroque] or *neobarroso* [*barroso*, or "murky"] art of the discard. The impoverished aesthetic of transvestites from the barrio commands its price when it exhibits the cheapness of the "nearly new," when its party dress is a women's garment taken from North American used clothing stores. Discarded clothing, an excess of the market destined for resale on the periphery (consumerism's leftovers), is recuperated by Latin American transvestites who dramatize their bastard luck by combining the syntactic remains of imported languages (gringo clothing) with their own disfigurative and transfigurative illusions, culminating in an endless copy of the copy. The North American garment—in disuse and then reused —anticipates in its discounted price the fall of certain models (subliminally: high fashion) once their facsimiles appear on the streets. Latin American transvestites, fluttering in the middle of a wardrobe-based syntagm of used clothing in order to conjoin a secondhand femininity, put the final touch on their parade of caricatures through the glorious imitation of a loaned femininity at once *copied* and *copy-catting*. The body-simulacrum (as Latino and false woman) of the poor transvestite, this trafficker in appearances, recycles on the Latin American periphery fragments (the detached garments of the North American sewing market) of a transferable pose that imitates the imitations of Joan Collins on *Dynasty*. That pose sets up the trans-mimetic crossing in which masterful reproductions and originals meet in carnivalized decadence, through the eccentric madness of disassembling *remnants of gender*, remnants and genders.‡

FIVE

Feminism and Postmodernism

A first obstacle to bringing together these two fields of discourse, postmodernism and feminism, is the variety of definitions and situations confusedly associated with each term. Postmodernism mixes theories and styles, modes and fashions, that indiscriminately traverse academic disciplines, everyday aesthetics, and market politics, promiscuously conjugating context-specific meanings that can be interpreted either as "reaction" (the neoconservative return to a fetishization of the capitalist order) or "resistance" (the resurgence of new forms of critical interference that challenge social and cultural officialism).

In the case of feminism, "what began as vindication in the face of the exclusion and devaluation of women, rapidly has evolved into a plurality of programs: liberal feminism, radical feminism, and socialist feminism."[1] And also into a variety of theoretical options that extend from essentialist and cultural feminism to poststructuralist and deconstructionist feminism.[2]

The second obstacle for us is that the theoretical debates articulating and engaging the range of postmodernist and feminist variants are debates marked by international metropolitan thought; they therefore must be reworked to serve the ends of local self-representation in order to oppose Euro–North American theory's centralizing paradigm.

Postmodernist Debate and Strategic Uses
of the Symptomatology of the Crisis

Several Latin American feminists deem it inappropriate to think in terms of modernity/postmodernity since we did not participate in the situation that gave rise to the origin and formulation of the crisis of modernity in the postindustrial contexts where that crisis was registered as discourse and theory.[3] It is true that we have not been integrated, or only in flawed ways, into the conceptualization and materialization of dominant European modernity's design, either as gender (woman) or as cultural identity (Latin America). It is also true that we have never been "strong" subjects in a tradition whose devaluation is dramatized by a Western philosophy that today laments the fall of the exclusive and excluding privileges of its universal metalanguage. But I don't believe that not fitting historically or geographically within the discursive parameter through which the postmodern crisis diagnoses and formulates its commentaries should deprive us of the opportunity to speak out about the ambiguities of registers generated by such a crisis, taking advantage of its most flexible figures.

Postmodern discourse emerges from the interior of a culture that always sought to administer, in a linear fashion, a consecutive sequence of "pres" and "posts" from the *unique* point of view of its dominant historic rationality. Today these abusive points of view have culminated in the postmodern operation of a metropolitan synthesis of economic and cultural power, a synthesis expressed by multinational capitalism in a series of combinations on a planetary scale. But postmodernist discourse, like every discourse, also presents discontinuities, flights of enunciation that enable us to make tactical use of its fractured perspectives in favor of a critical (Latin American) refunctionalization of the most insurgent vocabularies to emerge from the accounts of the crisis.[4]

Some postmodern enunciations already indirectly shed light on some of *our own* zones of cultural tension, not verbalized until now, or lacking in eloquence due to their not yet having faced questions that would call on them to be so intensively marked and unmarked. Such is the case with various zones of contradiction that form *folds* in the discourse of Latin American modernity. A first postmodern suggestion incites us to reread modernity from what it negates, or from what in its interior resists the classic guidance of pure luminous rationality: that which is hidden in the most shadowed zones of its "irrational rationality" [*razón desrazonable*] (Buci-Glucksmann). From the outset, these rereadings favor a perception of Latin American modernity as the plural interplay of uneven rationalities. And they thereby bring us closer to a *heterodox* understanding of the Latin American periphery's residual modernity: a modernity that joins and divides heterogeneous spaces and times, multistratified by discordant tendencies (myth and progress, orality and telecommunications, folklore and industry, traditions and the market, rites and simulacra). A modernity, then, whose grafts and transplants of disparate signs make it approximate more closely the *impurity* of the collage (and its play of dissimilar textures and surfaces) than the *purity* of an ethico-religious rituality that could remain as an uncontaminated *base* because it "maintained its nucleus of original values without modification."[5]

Another postmodern unearthing of these zones of "irrational rationality" teaches us that "the archeology of the modern has been obsessed with the feminine," with the baroque metaphor of an alterity and heterogeneity that always threatened to destabilize the "I" or identity of classic rationalism.[6] It is because of this that in each phase of the crisis, together with "the problem of modernity," the problem of woman and the "feminization of culture" reappears. That other zone of modernity's plural negativity, reaccentuated by postmodernity's critical inflection, is useful in analyzing "a series of correlations to be constructed between the culture of the crisis . . . , the deconstruction of the classic, conscious male subject, and the questioning of the masculine/feminine binary."[7]

But we must move beyond the benefits suggested by postmodern rereadings of modernity which celebrate the mixtures and jumblings of the hybrid languages of Latin American transculturation, or that unwind the baroque twists of the hidden fold of the "feminine." We must also argue in favor of another critical potential that justifies the peripheral transfer and recontextualization of one of postmodernism's themes: the theme of decentering and alterity.

The antiauthoritarian modulations of a new way of thinking drawn to the explosion and pulverization of categories like system, center, and hierarchy have transformed the figure of the *margin* into one of maximum critical tension. This figure makes use of the postmodern idea about the *dehierarchization of the center* (or of the Center's images) to redistribute the values between the canonical and the anticanonical, the dominant and minority, the hegemonic and subaltern, and so on, in favor of what up until now had been discarded or diminished by the official culture's (logocentric, phallocentric, Eurocentric, etc.) hierarchies. The fact that "the position of women is structurally and politically inscribed" in the marks of "absence, the periphery, the Other" has convinced several postmodern theorists that "feminism is the paradigmatic political discourse of postmodernism."[8]

Undoubtedly, Latin American feminism must remain watchful, generating resistance to the ways in which Euro–North American theory tends to vindicate the figure of the Other in order to *administer its own rhetoric* as international privilege: the decentered center speaks in representation of the Other, but generally does so while denying its own *others* (from the periphery) the opportunity to fight those mechanisms of discursive/institutional intervention and confrontation that would constitute and institute them as *subjects*, not objects of the discourse of otherness.[9] But along with remaining vigilant with regard to the stratagems of that "aestheticizing margino-centrality" [*marginocentralidad estetizante*] (Yúdice), Latin American feminism must also investigate which grooves and interstices of metropolitan theory could be used to twist or deviate the paradigm of the Other in *its favor*. It must also investigate which alliances of solidarity can and must be coordinated between certain peripheral discourses and certain metropolitan theories: those willing to explore the cartography of an "alternative postmodernity"[10] capable of crossing the prede-signed borders of official postmodernism.

In this sense, attempting crossovers between the postmodernism debate and feminism is not only an exciting task but a necessary one, since these crossovers are comprised of discussions vital to Latin American feminism: discussions about identity and power (about margins and centers; about the centering, decentering, and recenter-ing of cultural power), but also about theoretical-political strategies for inscribing difference (woman, periphery) into the problematic of "Difference," as a form of *dialoguing with*, and at the same time *inter-pellating*, postmodern theorizations of the Other validated in interna-tional centers.

True, many of postmodernism's official commentators did not try hard enough to safeguard lines of critique opposed to the conserva-tive recuperation of the cultural institution, an operation that availed itself of the antimodernist slogan of the death of the avant-gardes in order to return to the idealist-bourgeois tradition of academic cul-ture. It is also easy to show that commonplaces regarding the failure of utopian radicalism and revolutionary ideologism, discrediting the militant left, often operate as an alibi to celebrate a return to a social real now free of critical interventions and reconverted into the object of narcissistic contemplation. The same postmodern motto of the plural (plurality and pluralism) often conceals the neutralization of judgment that leads differences to passively serve the conformist in-difference of the "anything goes" liberalized by the market of goods and messages.

But together with the demobilizing charge of the skeptical rela-tivism and contemplative nihilism that characterize a particular post-modern style, tendencies exist within the same postmodernist field whose confrontational energy redeploys projects of sociocritical in-tervention. And more than lament or condemn those postmodern formulations (perhaps the most showy) that serve as an ideological disguise to the market moves of multinational capitalism, or that function as perverse allies to neoliberalism's shift to the right, we should "try to salvage the postmodern from its assumed total col-lusion with neoconservatism wherever possible; and [we should] explore the question whether postmodernism might not harbor productive contradictions, perhaps even a critical and oppositional potential. If the postmodern is indeed a historical and cultural condition (however transitional or incipient), then oppositional cultural practices and strategies must be located *within* postmodernism, not necessarily in its gleaming façades."[11]

The postmodern register emerges from the crisis of totalizing metanarratives based on the linear configuration subject-reason-science-progress characterizing modern philosophical and historical thought. That crisis can be interpreted—and it behooves us to do so—as produced by the fracturing of the authority of the omnipotent rationality of universal modernity's transcendental subject. It can be interpreted as a zone where the *grands récits* of modern epistemology—whose mission to found the absolute subject of sovereign truth today appears debilitated—break down.

Postmodernity as the register of "a crisis of cultural authority, specifically of the authority vested in Western European culture and its institutions,"[12] presupposes calling into question several notions on which the supremacy of a particular model of cultural identity has been based: a model based on omnicomprehensive totalizations of finite social and historical explanatory systems. The notions of *totality* (the freestanding fragment replaces the completeness of the Whole), of *centrality* (there is no longer a fixed point that can justify the superior dominion of an absolute reference), of *unity* (the monological paradigm of the One has been challenged by the disperse heterogeneity of the multiple) have all entered into crisis.

When postmodernity theorizes the fracturing of modernity's universal rationality—which had rendered absolute the Western-dominant subject as the sole possessor of knowledge—it in fact dismantles the representational archetypes whose authority was based on the primacy of the white-male-lettered-metropolitan subject. The delegitimation and dehierarchization of that colonial subject offers new signifying and participatory opportunities to identities and practices until then censured by the absolute truth of Western-masculine representation,[13] marginal identities and practices that oppose the central culture's hegemonic alliances in order to destabilize its dominant point of view. Woman and periphery, with their respective points of debate (feminism, Third Worldism, postcolonialism), form part of that theoretical-cultural landscape of new expressions that have nothing to lose—and much to gain—from the erosion and breaks in universal modernity's normative identity.

The postmodern problematic of "the other" can be *sharpened* by taking advantage of the fissures generated in the center's system of cultural authority and thought. In midst of the flow of proposals emanating from metropolitan culture, discerning those already open to a discussion of their authoritarian vices attests to a selective ability that favors the periphery, providing it with the raw material to thus *redirect* the meaning of the center's flaws. In this sense, the disintegration of dominant European modernity's totalizing paradigms stimulates the construction of alternative and dissident forms, whose oppositional potential must be embraced by the periphery despite the pretext that such paradigms were designed, theoretically, from the center. The postmodernist discourse of the decentered subject can be rearticulated in the margins' new poetics and politics, which encourage subaltern voices to take the canon of cultural authority by surprise, gaining support from the conflicting points of view unleashed at the center by social actors who denounce and contest the dominant narratives of superior culture. The critical potential of these new positions, which rebel against the regime of institutional limits and destabilize its hegemonic repertoire, must be harnessed and reinterpreted by the cultural periphery in its dispute with the center's reterritorializations.

Feminism of Equality and Feminism of Difference(s)

The relationship between feminism and the changing scenes of modernity/postmodernity is often described as a shift between a feminism of "equality"—conceived as emancipatory from the historical matrix of a modernity founded on the vector of social progress as guarantor of human justice—and a feminism of "difference"—that responds in a postmodern way to the disbelief in the universal (modern) paradigm of Identity as a historical and philosophical meta-reference.

But feminism of "difference" is not a set of positions harmonized in defense of commonly agreed-on postmodern arguments. A variety of contradictory meanings of "difference" exist that distinguish the various feminisms grouped under its name.[14] One could speak of

— Difference as *differences among women*, which seeks to correct the ahistorical tendency of some feminisms to represent Woman without specifying the experiential variables (race, ethnicity, class) that diversify each group beyond gender coordinates
— Difference as *the difference between men and women* (biological-sexual difference culturally reinterpreted through the mark of gender), a difference based on the division-opposition between masculinity and femininity taken as *separate* models of experience and culture
— Difference as the *relational and positional constructions of identity*, a difference that indicates masculinity and femininity as *modes* of subjective construction and strategies for critical manipulation of cultural and symbolic codes of identification and representation

While these three meanings coexist beneath the designation "feminism of difference," the term predominantly connotes an anti-essentialist and deconstructive feminism: a feminism that insistently has turned to psychoanalysis, semiotics, and deconstruction, in this way contradicting radical feminism's well-known mistrust of theory, considered an apparatus of male domination. This feminism of "difference" takes as its point of departure the postmetaphysical assumption that identity no longer constitutes the all-encompassing and unified reference of a transcendental idealism but rather the arena where psychic and social forces intersect, *decentering* the fiction of a transparent, selfsame "I." From the perspective of this poststructuralist feminism, the ruptures and disintegrations of the Unitary subject make it impossible to continue thinking of femininity as a fixed and constant value of homogenous substance. Rather than pursuing the feminine as *interiority*, this feminism proceeds to reflect on the exteriority of *signs* (representations) that socially construct and transmit the images of femininity with which subjects shape their identities, through repetition or negation, extracting and selecting roles and forms of subjectivity from the multiple, changing repertoires of culture.

But the theoretical validity of these feminine-gendered redefinitions of "identity," now construed as "difference," cannot cancel out the historical meaning of feminist struggles for sexual equality. In the words of Derrida:

> If we choose the egalitarian feminism, of the Enlightenment, . . . if we adhere to it, we will reproduce a culture that tends to erase difference, that measures the progress of women's condition simply against the condition of men. We thus will remain on the surface of professional, social, and political conditions, ending up finally in a sort of internalization of the masculine model. But if we limit ourselves to a feminism of difference we also risk reproducing a hierarchy, neglecting the forms of political, trade-union, professional struggle on the pretext that women, in their difference and to affirm their sexual difference, need not compete with men on all these levels.[15]

The relationships between feminism of "equality" and feminism of "difference" signal, then, a field of complex tensions between the various efforts that simultaneously orient and divide today's feminist problematic:

1. The effort to continue making progress in the political and social struggle to overcome forms of inequality that continue to oppress women at various levels of patriarchal domination = the struggle for equality.
2. The effort not to sacrifice, in the name of equality between men and women, the specificity and difference of the feminine, since the elimination of that profile subsumes women within the general category of the human and thereby disempowers (by neutralizing) their critique of the universal-masculine = vindication of difference.

3. The effort to avoid the separatism of "difference" that isolates women's culture as a culture *apart*, and that furthermore reessentializes the absolute feminine, leaving the system of polarized identities untouched = rejection of the identity/difference opposition and *multiplication of differences* as "differences that confound, disrupt and render ambiguous the meaning of any fixed binary opposition."[16]

The complexity of this game of critical operations which assemble and disassemble one another suggests that feminism's new political strategies should learn to combine and to alternate among these efforts, always strategically judging "the utility of certain arguments" (in favor of equality, difference, or differences) "in certain discursive contexts," without this entailing the invocation of "absolute qualities for women or men."[17]

This relativization of the categories man and woman, conceptualized not as fixed substances but rather as mobile constructs, is perhaps that which, among feminism's theoretical reformulations, best synchronizes with certain postmodern postulates: those related to the pluralization of meaning, the fragmentation of identity, and the dissemination of power.

Pluralization of meaning: History and society as texts stopped obeying a transcendental meaning subordinating comprehension of the real to its sole register of hierarchical reading, so that signs could proliferate and be disseminated horizontally in provisional and transitory signifying plots. Fragmentation of identity: Metaphysical rationality's self-possessed subject—homogenous and transparent—disintegrated into several "I's" that unsteadily combine plural marks of social, cultural, and sexual identification. Dissemination of power: There is no longer a homogenous polarity or fixed representation that locates power in *one* center, but rather there exist diffuse networks which multiply and disperse their points of antagonism and lines of confrontation.

This detotalization of the categories sign, culture, and power invites feminism to reformulate its antipatriarchal critique with the support of new "theories that will let us think in terms of pluralities and diversities rather than of unities and universals,"[18] allying itself to this end with those postmodern formulations that critique the monological identities of totalizing rationality.

A certain feminist appropriation of poststructuralist theory emphasizes "identity" as *construction, positionality*, and *relationality*. That is, as the active transformation of the basic facts of corporal biography through cultural symbolizations that are changing and changeable and that revoke the sustaining postulate of an identity self-defined once and for all.

Taken to an extreme, this deessentializing tendency raised the fear that the abandonment of gender difference (sexuality) in favor of the feminine as *subject position* (textuality) would prove completely deactivating to feminist consciousness raising and its desire for social change: if women exist only abstractly as articulations of signs and discursive positionalities, and not concretely as a gender, there would be nothing to fight for in the name of their liberation from the material as well as symbolic violence of patriarchy.[19] But the vindication of the subject, as discursive position and strategy, need not detach itself from the material analysis of the conditions of signification and power in which the *politics of identity* — concretely — are articulated and dismantled. Huyssen writes: "The question of how codes, texts, images and other cultural artifacts constitute subjectivity is increasingly being raised as an always already historical question,"[20] and also a gendered one. There is no reason to assume that emphasizing the *positionality* of the feminine (in the *play of locations* of the sign of sexual difference, whose mobility exceeds the ontological assumptions associated with the "body" as referent) necessarily entails the degenderization of sexual difference. It is possible to combine, in their respective levels of efficacy, the effort to continue mobilizing gender as a platform for social vindication based on the signifier "woman" with the other effort to challenge the codes of symbolic and interpretive power from a mobile plurality of critical subject positions-postures that propel the constellation of "minority instantiations" of the "feminine."

To take on the question of the feminine, no longer as the expression of an "I" in possession of the representation of a total and absolute femininity (by biographic-corporal extraction) but rather as a *problematic of subjectivity*, forces feminism to work on a theoretical articulation that recognizes each subject as traversed by a conflicting multiplicity of identifying impulses and logics of power. Only a feminism that theorizes the feminine as a force of intervention in the politic(s) of identity will respond to the necessity "in neocolonial countries of studying the subjection of women in terms of global relationships of power."[21]

This characterizes the Latin American context because there are always various mechanisms of oppression and repression (colonialist, neo-imperialist, militaristic and patriarchal, multicapitalist, etc.) weaving themselves *diagonally*: masculine-patriarchal ideology traverses subjects, discourses, and institutions, creating nodes with other devices of power (through intersections and superimpositions) which become combined in mixed enunciatory formations. It is the imbrication of these multiple figures-of-the-system that must be delved into since the points of greatest symbolic violence are those saturated by the coactive exercise of several logics of domination that reinforce and enable one another. The movement from one figure to another in order to disentangle the webs of tacit complicity binding different enunciations, implies that the "feminine" should be deployed with the greatest plurality of critical movements in order to dismantle the machinery of rationalities and powers that seek, among other things, to tie us to fixed categorizations of homogenous identities: the feminine identity, the Latin American identity, and so on. Refuting these categorizations not only makes sense for theoretical analysis. We confirm daily that "there are too many female breadwinners, male nurturers, feminist housewives and mothers, white, middle-class males teaching black, feminist literature, in short, too many transgressions or confusions of gender in our everyday engagements."[22] Not only do they make us feel that the old, absolute discourses of masculinity and femininity have become anachronistic; they also demand that we reformulate "the normative content of feminist argument"[23] in function of that multipositionality of the subject that has begun to take concrete forms through the actual diversification and increased complexity of social and gender roles rubbing against the divisive boundaries and ranks of traditionally constituted identities. A denormativizing reformulation of militant feminism's battle cry that also would allow dimensions like creativity, fantasy, pleasure, taste, and style to mix *aesthetic impulses* with the *will to change* in order to intertwine the figural and strategic repertoires of *seduction* and *sedition*.

Notes

Translators' Preface

1 For commentary on Richard's work within the context of Southern Cone culture after 1990, see Francine Masiello, *The Art of Transition: Latin American Culture and Neoliberal Crisis* (Durham, N.C.: Duke University Press, 2001).

2 Nelly Richard, *Residuos y metáforas: Ensayos de crítica cultural sobre el Chile de la transición* [Residues and metaphors: Essays of cultural criticism on Chile during the transition] (Santiago: Editorial Cuarto Propio, 1998), 13–14. All translations from this text are our own. A translation of this work is forthcoming from the University of Minnesota Press.

3 Ibid., 23.

4 Ibid.

5 Ana del Sarto, "Cultural Critique in Latin America or Latin-American Cultural Studies?" *Journal of Latin American Cultural Studies* 9, 3 (2000): 236.

6 For in-depth studies of Nelly Richard's work and its role in the development of Latin American cultural studies, consult the first five articles in the *Journal of Latin American Cultural Studies* 9, 3 (2000).

7 Other works by Richard in English translation include: "Margins and Institutions: Art in Chile since 1973," special issue of *Art & Text* 21 (1986); her "Reply to Vidal (from Chile)," in *The Postmodernism Debate in Latin America*, ed. John Beverley and José Oviedo (Durham, N.C.: Duke University Press, 1993), 228–31; and "Chile, Women, and Dissidence" (137–44), "Women's Art Practices and the Critique of Signs" (145–51), and "Postmodern Decentrednesses and Cultural Periphery: The Disalignments and Realignments of Cultural Power" (260–69), in *Beyond the Fantastic: Contem-*

porary Art Criticism in Latin America, ed. Gerardo Mosquera (Cambridge: MIT Press, 1996).

8   Michel de Certeau, "Preface to the English Translation," in *The Practice of Everyday Life*, trans. Steven Rendall (Berkeley: University of California Press, 1984), ix.

ONE   *Spatial Politics*

1   Barbero, *Procesos de comunicación*, 45.

2   "This would entail being attentive to that which is less visible, less audible, discourses and practices that, through fissures, already escape market determinism, habitual circuits. But it also entails differentiating that which in the market works against its rules, poses the unforeseeable questions, imagines new models of response. . . . To discover the forms and itineraries through which the discourse of art questions the very place adjudicated to it, the order in which it is integrated, overflowing the limits of what has been possible up to now and sketching, figuratively, perhaps utopianly, the future forms of a system of relationships. Upon thwarting the expectations and subverting the standards of the foreseeable, discursive fragments demand to be heard differently, anticipate what still remains obscure in society, or shed a different light on a past that seemed definitively organized." Sarlo, "Una mirada política," 3.

3   For reference material on this debate, see the issue "Cultura, política y democracia" of the *Revista de crítica cultural* 5 (1992).

4   "What for classic Marxism was the homogenous space of the working class today reveals itself to us as the combination and unstable articulation of a plurality of subject positions. . . . Each social agent is penetrated by a multiplicity of subject positions that find no necessary binding core in the positioning of that agent within relationships of production. . . . One can perfectly imagine a society in which private ownership of the means of production has been eliminated and in which, nevertheless, the repression of homosexuals and subordination of women continue fully in force. That is, if the different aspects of the socialist ideal—let's call it that for the moment—are to be realized, they must be the result of the specific mobilization of each one of those groups interested in diverse vindications." Laclau, *Materiales de krítica*.

5   That "new scene" brought together a group of practices in which "unusual proposals in the literary and visual arenas were generated. Writers and artists, in close interrelationship, attempted to offer a language that . . .

counterposing both its recent past and the order imposed by the domina-
tor . . . operated from a decentering, from dispersion, from impulses, from
the annihilation of unity." Brito, *Campos minados*, 8.

6   One of these attempts at a dialogue was recorded in Richard et al.,
Arte en Chile desde 1973: Escena de avanzada y sociedad.

7   Some of the tensions between artistic-literary neo–avant-garde,
militant culture and alternative sociology were analyzed in Richard, "El
signo heterodoxo," 102–11.

8   For a perspective on the feminist problematic in the context of the
democratic transition, see Olea, "La redemocratización," 30–32.

9   I refer the reader particularly to Kirkwood, *Ser política en Chile.*

10   The Jornadas de la Mujer [Women's Work Days] that took place in
the Centro Cultural Mapocho (Santiago) in November 1982 constituted one
of the few attempts to join social practices and cultural discourses through
reflection in the workshops. On the other hand, and as a testament to the
audacity of the gestures realized by the artistic neo–avant-garde, Diamela
Eltit and Lotty Rosenfeld (members of the group CADA) opted to respond to
the invitation extended to them by the Círculo de la Mujer [Women's Circle]
to participate in the commemoration of International Women's Day with
"the exhibition of a pornographic film that consisted of a triangle config-
ured by a *patrona* [matron], a female servant, and a dog" and with "a textual
analysis of that film" (published in *Ruptura* [Santiago, August 1982]). Their
analysis of how "the masculine presence" only materializes in "the camera-
work and direction of the film, including and orienting the taping" enabled
the authors to say that, "with the pretext of 'femininity,' this film makes
evident the real denotative circuit that masks all social organization: the act
of penetration occurs only between men."

11   Lizama, *Los nuevos espacios de la política*, 79.

12   Olea, "El lugar de Gabriela Mistral," 18.

13   Grau, "Presentación," 14.

14   Ibid. Among those activities realized in university spaces, I should
highlight: the sequence of presentations and talks organized by the Casa
de la Mujer La Morada that took place at the Universidad Nacional Andrés
Bello ("Ver desde la mujer, ver a la mujer" [To see from the position of
women, to see women], September 1990); the Interdisciplinary Program in
Women's Studies begun in 1991 at the Universidad de Concepción; the seminar "Women and Anthropology: Problematics and Perspectives," organized
in March 1992 by the anthropology department of the Universidad de Chile
and the Centro de Estudios para el Desarrollo de la Mujer [Center of Studies

for Women's Development] (CEDEM); and the seminar entitled "Education and Gender," organized by the Casa de la Mujer La Morada (August 1992) at the Universidad Metropolitana de Ciencias de la Educación.

15 Adriana Valdés, presentation on the book *Ver desde la mujer* at the Universidad Metropolitana (August 1992).

16 For example, in his talk, "Historia de la mujer en Chile: Historia de géneros: Apuntes para un balance preliminar," Víctor Toledo warns that in the field of historiography, the vast majority of research taking the subject of women as its thematic focus "remains located in the framework of a history already defined by structural lines and periodizations, according to androcentric approaches and/or a traditional interpretation of history articulated from a position of power, whether positivist or Marxist, etc. Left unquestioned is the general interpretation of the history of a given period or process. New facts and female names are added, but the dimensions, the interpretive gaze, remain unaltered." Paper presented at the seminar "Women and Anthropology."

17 Olea, "Más sobre mujer y escritura," 2–3.

18 Rossanda, "Nuestras perlas escondidas," 123–24.

19 Bakhtin speaks of how "at any given moment of its historical existence, language is heteroglot from top to bottom: it represents the coexistence of socio-ideological contradictions between . . . these 'languages' of heteroglossia." Bakhtin, "Discourse in the Novel," in *The Dialogic Imagination: Four Essays*, 291.

20 Derrida, "Feminismo y de(s)construcción," 26.

21 Kirkwood, *Ser política en Chile*, 201.

22 In her talk, "Proposición de paradigmas para la comprensión del género en América Latina," Sonia Montecino claims that "to render explicit the mix of theories and models, and the fragmentary use we make of them, may constitute an 'other' way of knowing." Paper presented at the seminar "Women and Anthropology."

23 Foucault, "Respuesta a *Esprit*," 71.

24 Rossanda, "Nuestras perlas escondidas," 136–37.

25 Ortega, *El discurso de la abundancia*, 256.

TWO *Does Writing Have a Gender?*

1 This conference was co-organized by Carmen Berenguer (Chile), Diamela Eltit (Chile), Lucía Guerra (United States), Eliana Ortega (Chile), and Nelly Richard (Chile). Its proceedings were published in Berenguer et al., *Escribir en los bordes*.

* *Translators' note:* In this essay, Richard enters into dialogue with con-temporary French feminist debates on women's writing and *écriture feminine*. In engaging with that literature, we have rendered key terms as follows: *escritura*-"*mujer*" and *escritura de mujeres* as *women's writing*; *literatura de mujeres* as *literature by women*; *escritura femenina* as *feminine writing*; and *literatura femenina* as *women's literature*.

2   In *Campos minados*, Brito writes: "It was after the first Conference on Latin American Women's Literature that women writers, especially the poets, slowly became aware of the complicitous silence registered even by leftists, even by the very best writers and critics, toward women's writing" (73).

3   Raquel Olea lucidly analyzes the problematic of the *inscription* of feminist literary criticism in the Chilean cultural milieu in her "Más sobre mujer y escritura," 2–3.

4   This space for feminist literary criticism in Chile was developed gradually by members of a few working groups. I should mention among them: the literary and feminist criticism workshop directed by Mercedes Valdivieso at the Círculo de Estudios de la Mujer [Women's Study Circle] in November 1983, with the participation of Adriana Valdés, Sonia Monte-cino, Cecilia Sánchez, Diamela Eltit, Nelly Richard, and others; the work-shop "Lectura de mujeres" [Women's reading group], directed by Raquel Olea, Eliana Ortega, Soledad Fariña, and Teresa Adriasola, and organized by the Casa de la Mujer La Morada, which sponsored a conference on the poet Gabriela Mistral, with proceedings published as *Una palabra cómplice: Encuentro con Gabriela Mistral*; the workshop developed simultaneously with the preparation of the Conference on Latin American Women's Literature (1987), with the participation of Diamela Eltit, Eugenia Brito, Raquel Olea, Nelly Richard, and others; and Kemy Oyarzún's course "Latin American Feminist Literary Theory," offered in the department of philosophy and lit-erature at the Universidad de Chile in January 1992.

5   Olea, "Más sobre mujer y escritura," 2.

6   Bianchi, "Lectura de mujeres," 126.

7   Sabaj, "Texto, cuerpo, mujer," 3.

8   Ibid.

9   Ibid.

10   I draw on these questions from Marta Contreras's review of Marina Arrate's *Este lujo de ser*, published in *Revista LAR* 11, a special edition entitled "Women and Writing" in August 1987.

11   The citation is Hélène Cixous's, extracted from Adriana Méndez's article "Tradición y escritura femenina," 85.

12   The translation of this citation is from Jean-François Lyotard, "Féminité dans la métalangue," 213–14.

13   Ludmer, "El espejo universal," 275–76.

14   See especially Kristeva's *Revolution in Poetic Language* and *Polylogue*, whose contents form part of the English collection *Desire in Language*.

15   Eltit, "Cultura, poder y frontera," 2.

16   Bianchi, "Lectura de mujeres," 128.

17   Eltit, responses published in the previously cited special edition of *Revista LAR* 11 (1987).

18   Kuhn, *Women's Pictures*, 18.

19   The citation comes from Sandra M. Gilbert and Susan Gubar's *The Madwoman in the Attic*, as quoted in Valdés, "Una pregunta desde Chile."

20   Ibid.

21   Schopf, "Suplemento."

22   Valdés, "El espacio literario de la mujer en la colonia."

23   Franco, *Plotting Women*, xi.

24   Soledad Bianchi asked, "Aren't there still too many texts that corner their female characters in a limited domestic, private sphere, a doubtful feminine monopoly?" in her presentation "Escribir desde la mujer."

25   Schopf, "Suplemento."

26   Fariña, [untitled], 29.

27   Julia Kristeva, cited in Moi, *Sexual/Textual Politics*, 163. The citation comes from Kristeva's "Woman's Time."

28   See Jacqueline Rose's chapter "Femininity and Its Discontents," in *Sexuality in the Field of Vision*.

29   Mattelart, "Les femmes et l'ordre de la crise."

30   Eltit, *Lumpérica*, *Por la patria*, *El cuarto mundo*, *El padre mío*, and *Vaca sagrada*.

THREE *Politics and Aesthetics*

1   Pollock, *Vision and Difference*, 5.

2   I am referring to the exhibit *Chilenas*, coordinated by Cecilia Boisier and realized in Berlin's Kumstamt Kreuzberg (October–December 1983) and the exhibit *Mujer, arte y periferia*, organized by Diamela Eltit, Lotty Rosenfeld, and Nelly Richard in *Women in Focus* (November–December 1987) in Vancouver, British Columbia, Canada.

3   This designation covers that group of Chilean artistic and poetic-literary practices that distinguished themselves, starting in 1977, by the neo–avant-garde slant of their formal, technical, and linguistic experimen-

tation. [They also have been referred to as the *escena de avanzada*.] These practices were analyzed primarily in Richard, *Margins and Institutions* and in Brito, *Campos minados*.

    ★ *Translators' note*: In Chile, an *imbunche* is a witch or warlock, a raptor of children (according to the indigenous Mapuche tradition), or any deformed or malevolent being with supernatural powers. Parra plays with this concept to impugn the official press's "smoke and mirrors," employed in complicitous support of the military regime (and perhaps also to invoke art's power to cast spells).

    4 I refer the reader to Ronald Christ's brilliant analysis of Catalina Parra's oeuvre in his text "Images After the Word." Christ writes: "She says that she found the word was first for her; I say that she also found the word was everywhere, and that the word was her father's. . . . One—and I emphasize: *one*—motif and motive, then, in Parra's work conducts the struggle of word and image, which began in a child's failed attempt to replace word with image; really, to reverse their order. We may, if we choose, view this as the child's attempt to *displace* the father, absent but ubiquitous in the play of language" (35–37).

    5 "Rosenfeld utilizes as a model the discontinuous lines that separate the paths of circulation; a traffic mark which she crosses perpendicularly with a white mark identical to it, generating a series of plus (+) signs on the pavement." Brito et al., *Desacato*.

    † *Translators' note*: Maipú Street is in a marginal neighborhood in Santiago by the same name.

    6 "All the systems of exchange that organize patriarchal societies and all the modalities of productive work that are recognized, valued, and rewarded in these societies are men's business. . . . The work force is thus always assumed to be masculine, and 'products' are objects to be used, objects of transaction among men alone." Irigaray, *This Sex Which Is Not One*, 171.

    7 The precariousness of the "bad image" was the aesthetic defended by the photocopied text that accompanied the video *Materiales de cámara* [Camera materials] presented by Diamela Eltit and Lotty Rosenfeld at the Festival de Video organized by the Instituto Francés de Cultura [French Cultural Institute] in 1985.

    8 I am referring to the video festivals organized by the Instituto Francés de Cultura starting in 1980, which proved, for most of their run, to be one of the most polemic sites for critical discussion regarding visual strategies of filmed images.

    9 The exhibit *Mujeres en el arte* at the Museo Nacional de Bellas Artes [National Fine Arts Museum] in March 1991 was organized by SERNAM

(Servicio Nacional de la Mujer) [National Service for Women] to celebrate Women's Day. More than 120 Chilean artists participated.

10   Olhagaray, "Video Ready Made."

11   Sarlo, "Políticas culturales," 12.

12   "Cultural democracy today necessarily implies a communicative democracy. In other words, the possibility that the different social and cultural agents in the nation express themselves. That they be present in the collective imaginary: in the mode in which we conceive of and represent ourselves. Cultural plurality must be expressed through the mass media. This helps to favor the self-image and to democratize society in a sense beyond the strictly political. Only in the measure that the heterogeneity of sectors, groups, or latent cultural energies existing in society are recognized and favored (by the State, civil, or political society) will the bases for the full expression of each individual's creative movement be set." Subercaseaux, "Democratización y democracia cultural," 27.

13   The preference of certain feminists for these "anticlassical" languages is discussed by Gisela Breitling in "Speech, Silence, and the Discourse of Art," 162–63.

14   See Pollock, Vision and Difference, 156.

15   Along these lines, Craig Owens writes: "Because of the tremendous effort of reconceptualization necessary to prevent a phallologic relapse in their own discourse, many feminist artists have, in fact, forged a new (or renewed) alliance with theory. . . . Many modernist artists, of course, produced texts about their own production, but writing was almost always considered supplementary to their primary work as painters, sculptors, photographers, etc., whereas the kind of simultaneous activity on multiple fronts that characterizes many feminist practices is a postmodern phenomenon. And one of the things it challenges is modernism's rigid opposition of artistic practice and theory." Owens, "The Discourse of Others," 63.

16   The publication of Ruptura (1980), edited by CADA, is perhaps the best example of that interaction.

17   De Lauretis, Technologies of Gender, 130.

FOUR Gender Contortions

    *   Translators' note: While the Spanish term travesti means "transvestite" in English, the cultural contexts for the two terms require clarification. In the United States, transvestite does not communicate the gayness of the cross-dresser, while the term drag queen emphasizes both the person's gayness and the performative nature of her acts. However, Richard uses the

term *travesti* to speak of such drag queens (*locas* or madwomen), performers emphasizing their own gayness and gender play. We retain the term *transvestite* to follow Richard's usage and to be consistent with other literature on the artists discussed in this chapter. See, for example, Jean Franco's "The Mares of the Apocalypse," in *Critical Passions: Selected Essays*, ed. Mary Louise Pratt and Kathleen Newman (Durham, N.C.: Duke University Press, 1999), 109–22.

† *Translators' note*: We have conserved Richard's use of the terms *gay* and *homosexual*, but would note that her usage is similar to the ways in which U.S. scholarship has embraced the term *queer* to denote an array of challenges to rigid systems of gender and sexual identification.

1   Juan Dávila is a Chilean artist who has resided in Australia since 1979. He continued to exhibit his work regularly in Chile during the years of the military regime.

2   Marchant, "On the Use of Certain Words."

3   Juan Dávila and Carlos Leppe presented this performance video at the Instituto Francés de Cultura in Santiago in 1982. This work also included the video *The Bible*, by Martín Munz, presented at the Fourth Biennial in Sydney, also in 1982.

4   Marchant, "On the Use of Certain Words," 77. [Only the first half of this is quoted on page 77; the entire quotation appears in the original photocopied version of this text in Spanish.]

5   Ibid., 81.

6   Similarly, Guy Hocquenghem critiques the centrality of the Phallic Reference in heterosexism through the inverted gesture of resublimating the Anus, in *Homosexual Desire*.

7   Marchant, "On the Use of Certain Words," 81.

8   Ibid., 82 [Richard's emphasis].

9   For example, Juan Dávila's paintings multiply signatures by serializing the index of authors' names.

10   Bianchi, "Maquillaje para una carcajada triste," 11.

11   Donoso and Errázuriz, *La manzana de Adán*.

12   Eltit, "Una mirada en los intersticios," 31 (on Paz Errázuriz's work).

13   Perlongher, "Avatares de los muchachos de la noche."

14   Zurita, "Ernesto Muñoz."

15   Texts published by Pedro Lemebel in the magazine *Página abierta* during 1991–92, framed under the title "Crónica urbana" [Urban chronicles], also charted gay excursions, graphing positions in the city (from the Plaza de Armas in Santiago to movie theaters and the municipal park) within a clandestine map of libidinal undercurrents.

16 Lemebel, "Ojo con el Under," 33.

17 Zurita, "Ernesto Muñoz."

18 Lemebel, "Fertil providencia señalada," 14.

19 Olalquiaga, "Cultura buitresca," 10.

‡ *Translators' note:* Like the pun on *remnants*, Richard also plays on the word *género* here, which not only means "gender" and "genre" but also "cloth." So when she speaks of "remnants of gender," she also implies the bits of cloth involved in the transvestite's secondhand garments.

FIVE *Feminism and Postmodernism*

1 Franco, "Si me permiten hablar," 88.

2 Teresa de Lauretis refers to the Anglo-American feminist tendency of "typologizing, defining and branding various 'feminisms' along an ascending scale of theoretico-political sophistication where 'essentialism' weighs heavy at the lower end" (4); "essentialism as the belief in 'female nature' is associated with cultural feminism, 'separatist' feminism, radical feminism (with qualifications), and occasionally liberal feminism, while socialist feminism and now poststructuralist or deconstructive feminism come out at the top of the scale" (33 n, "The Essence of the Triangle").

3 As an example, I refer the reader to Raquel Olea's comment: "The modernity/postmodernity polemic cannot be the object of our feminist, Latin American discourse, whose ambiguous integration into the cultural processes proceeding from Eurocentrism impede even the possession of its own reality. . . . On the other hand, we women have been subjects neither of the modern project nor of its crisis." Fragment taken from her talk "Feminismo."

4 This argument is incorporated in my article "Latinoamérica y la postmodernidad."

5 From Morandé's *Ritual y palabra*, cited in Montecino, Dussuel, and Wilson, "Identidad femenina y modelo mariano en Chile," in *Mundo de mujer*, 505. For a counterpoint to Pedro Morandé's theses (taken up by Sonia Montecino), I refer the reader to José Joaquín Brunner's and Néstor García Canclini's reflections on the "cultural heterogeneity" or the "multitemporal heterogeneity" of Latin American modernity: Brunner, *Un espejo trizado*, and García Canclini, *Hybrid Cultures*.

6 Buci-Glucksmann, *La raison baroque*, 34.

7 Ibid., 33.

8 Kipnis, "Feminism," 160–61.

9 "What we must eliminate are systems of representation that carry

with them the kind of authority which, to my mind, has been repressive because it doesn't permit or make room for interventions on the part of those
represented. . . . The alternative would be a representational system that
was participatory and collaborative, non-coercive, rather than imposed, but
as you know, this is not a simple matter. We have no immediate access to
the means of producing alternative systems. Perhaps it would be possible
through other, less exploitative fields of knowledge. But first we must iden-
tify those social, cultural, political formations which would allow for a reduction of authority and increased participation in the production of representations, and proceed from there." Said, "In the Shadow of the West," 95.

10   Yúdice, "El conflicto de postmodernidades," 31.

11   Huyssen, "Mapping the Postmodern," 29.

12   Owens, "The Discourse of Others," 57.

13   Glimpsing these opportunities, however, should not make us forget
the following: "If one of the most salient aspects of our postmodern culture
is the presence of an insistent feminist voice . . . , theories of postmodernism
have tended either to neglect or to repress that voice. The absence of discussions of sexual difference in writings about postmodernism, as well as
the fact that few women have engaged in the modernism/postmodernism
debate, suggest that postmodernism may be another masculine invention
engineered to exclude women" (ibid., 61).

14   Barret, "The Concept of Difference."

15   Derrida, "Feminismo y de(s)construcción," 26.

16   Scott, "Deconstructing Equality-versus-Difference," 48.

17   Ibid., 47.

18   Ibid., 33.

19   The same thing occurs if one takes too seriously certain modernist-
postmodernist proclamations related to "the death of the subject," despite
the fact that they were formulated to combat the bourgeois idealism that
consecrated the metaphysical subject: we must, indeed, ask ourselves if
the commonplace regarding the "death of the subject" "isn't [jettisoning]
the chance of challenging the *ideology of the subject* (as male, white, and
middle-class) by developing alternative and different notions of subjectivity." Huyssen, "Mapping the Postmodern," 44.

20   Ibid.

21   Oyarzún, "Edipo, autogestión y producción textual," 593.

22   Soper, "Postmodernism and Its Discontents," 106.

23   Ibid.

Bibliography

Bakhtin, Mikhail M. *The Dialogic Imagination: Four Essays*. Ed. Michael Holquist. Trans. Caryl Emerson and Holquist. Austin: University of Texas Press, 1981.

Barbero, Jesús Martín. *Procesos de comunicación y matrices de cultura* [Communication processes and cultural matrices]. Mexico: Ediciones G. Gili, 1987.

Barret, Michèle. "The Concept of Difference." *Feminist Review* 26 (1987): 29–41.

Berenguer, Carmen, et al., eds. *Escribir en los bordes* [Writing in/on the margins]. Santiago: Editorial Cuarto Propio, 1990.

Bianchi, Soledad. "Escribir desde la mujer" [To write from the position of women]. Paper presented at the seminar "Culture, Authoritarianism, and Democratization in Chile," University of Maryland, College Park, December 1991.

———. "Lectura de mujeres" [Women's reading]. In *Ver desde la mujer* [To see from the position of women], ed. Olga Grau, 125–41. Santiago: Ediciones La Morada, Editorial Cuarto Propio, 1992.

———. "Maquillaje para una carcajada triste" [Make-up for a sad guffaw]. Prologue to *Sodoma mía* [Sodom-my], by Francisco Casas, 9–11. Santiago: Editorial Cuarto Propio, 1991.

Breitling, Gisela. "Speech, Silence, and the Discourse of Art." In *Feminist Aesthetics*, ed. Gisela Ecker, trans. Harriet Anderson, 162–74. Boston: Beacon, 1986.

Brito, Eugenia. *Campos minados: Literatura post-golpe en Chile* [Mined fields: Post-coup literature in Chile]. Santiago: Editorial Cuarto Propio, 1990.

Brito, Eugenia, et al. *Desacato: Sobre la obra de Lotty Rosenfeld* [Disrespect: On the work of Lotty Rosenfeld]. Santiago: Francisco Zegers Editor, 1986.

Brunner, José Joaquín. *Un espejo trizado: Ensayos sobre cultura y políticas culturales* [A shattered mirror: Essays on culture and cultural politics]. Santiago: Flacso, 1988.

Buci-Glucksmann, Christine. *La raison baroque: De Baudelaire à Benjamin* [Baroque reason: From Baudelaire to Benjamin]. Paris: Galilée, 1984.

Christ, Ronald. "Images after the Word." In *Catalina Parra in Retrospect*, ed. Julia P. Herzberg and Catalina Parra (Bronx, N.Y.: The Gallery, 1991).

Contreras, Marta. "Este lujo de ser" [This luxury of being]. Review of *Este lujo de ser*, by Marina Arrate. *LAR: Revista de literatura* 11 (1987): 59–60.

De Lauretis, Teresa. "The Essence of the Triangle; or, Taking the Risk of Essentialism Seriously: Feminist Theory in Italy, the U.S., and Britain." *differences* 1, 2 (1989): 3–37.

―――.*Technologies of Gender: Essays on Theory, Film, and Fiction*. Bloomington: Indiana University Press, 1987.

Derrida, Jacques. "Feminismo y de(s)construcción" [Feminism and deconstruction]. Interview by Cristina de Peretti. *Revista de crítica cultural* 3 (1991): 24–27.

Donoso, Claudia, and Paz Errázuriz. *La manzana de Adán* [Adam's apple]. Santiago: Editorial Zona, 1990.

Eltit, Diamela. "Cultura, poder y frontera" [Culture, power, and border]. *La época: Literatura y libros*, 10 June 1990, 1–2.

―――. *E. Luminata* [*Lumpérica*]. Trans. Ronald Christ. 1983. Santa Fe, N. Mex.: Lumen, 1997.

―――. *The Fourth World* [*El cuarto mundo*]. Trans. Dick Gerdes. 1988. Lincoln: University of Nebraska Press, 1995.

―――. "Una mirada en los intersticios" [A gaze from the interstices]. *Página abierta*, June–July 1992, 31.

―――. *El padre mío* [Father of mine]. Santiago: Francisco Zegers Editor, 1989.

―――. *Por la patria* [For the fatherland]. Santiago: Ediciones del Ornitorrinco, 1986.

―――. *Sacred Cow* [*Vaca sagrada*]. Trans. Amanda Hopkinson. 1991. New York: Serpent's Tail, 1995.

Eltit, Diamela, and Lotty Rosenfeld. "A Textual Analysis." *Ruptura*, August 1982.

Fariña, Soledad. [Untitled.] *LAR: Revista* 11 (1987): 29.

Foucault, Michel. "Respuesta a *Esprit*" [Response to *Esprit*]. In *Michel Foucault: El discurso del poder* [Michel Foucault: The discourse of power], ed. and trans. Oscar Terán, 64–87. Buenos Aires: Ediciones Folios, 1983.

Franco, Jean. *Plotting Women: Gender and Representation in Mexico.* New York: Columbia University Press, 1989.

————. "Si me permiten hablar: La lucha por el poder interpretativo" [If you allow me to speak: The struggle for interpretive power]. *Casa de las Américas* 171 (1988): 88–94.

García Canclini, Néstor. *Hybrid Cultures: Strategies for Entering and Leaving Modernity.* Trans. Christopher L. Chiappari and Silvia L. López. Minneapolis: University of Minnesota Press, 1995.

Grau, Olga. "Presentación" [Presentation]. In *Ver desde la mujer* [To see from the position of women], ed. Grau, 11–17. Santiago: Ediciones La Morada, Editorial Cuarto Propio, 1992.

Hocquenghem, Guy. *Homosexual Desire.* Trans. Daniella Dangoor. London: Allison and Busby, 1978.

Huyssen, Andreas. "Mapping the Postmodern." *New German Critique* 33, (1984): 5–52.

Irigaray, Luce. *This Sex Which Is Not One.* Trans. Catherine Porter with Carolyn Burke. Ithaca, N.Y.: Cornell University Press, 1985.

Kipnis, Laura. "Feminism: The Political Conscience of Postmodernism?" In *Universal Abandon? The Politics of Postmodernism,* ed. Andrew Ross, 149–66. Minneapolis: University of Minnesota Press, 1988.

Kirkwood, Julieta. *Ser política en Chile: Las feministas y los partidos* [Being a political woman in Chile: Feminists and the parties]. Santiago: Editorial Cuarto Propio, 1990.

Kristeva, Julia. *Desire in Language: A Semiotic Approach to Literature and Art.* Ed. Leon S. Roudiez. Trans. Thomas Gora, Alice Jardine, and Roudiez. New York: Columbia University Press, 1980.

————. *Polylogue* [Polylogue]. Paris: Éditions du Seuil, 1977.

————. *Revolution in Poetic Language.* Trans. Margaret Waller. New York: Columbia University Press, 1984.

Kuhn, Annette. *Women's Pictures: Feminism and Cinema.* Boston: Routledge and Kegan Paul, 1982.

Laclau, Ernesto. Interview in *Materiales de krítica* 2 (1986).

Lemebel, Pedro. "Fertil providencia señalada" [Fertile appointed providence]. *Página abierta,* November 1991, 14.

————. "Ojo con el Under" [Watch out for what's Down Under]. *Página abierta,* March 1992, 33.

Lizama, Jaime. *Los nuevos espacios de la política* [The new spaces of politics]. Santiago: Ediciones Documentas, 1991.

Ludmer, Josefina. "El espejo universal y la perversión de la fórmula" [The universal mirror and the perversion of the formula]. In *Escribir en los bordes*

[Writing in/on the margins], ed. Carmen Berenguer et al., 275–87. Santiago: Editorial Cuarto Propio, 1990.

Lyotard, Jean-François. "Féminité dans la métalangue" [Femininity in metalanguage]. In *Rudiments païens: Genre dissertatif*, 213–32. Paris: Union Générale d'Éditions, 1977.

Marchant, Patricio. "On the Use of Certain Words." Trans. Ron Keightley. *Art & Text* 9 (1983): 72–83.

Mattelart, Michèle. "Les femmes et l'ordre de la crise" [Women and the order of the crisis]. *Tel quel* 74 (1977): 9–23.

Méndez Rodenas, Adriana. "Tradición y escritura femenina" [Tradition and feminine writing]. In *Escribir en los bordes* [Writing in/on the margins], ed. Carmen Berenguer et al., 85–102. Santiago: Editorial Cuarto Propio, 1990.

Moi, Toril. *Sexual/Textual Politics: Feminist Literary Theory*. London: Methuen, 1985.

Montecino, Sonia. "Proposición de paradigmas para la comprensión del género en América Latina" [A proposal of paradigms for understanding gender in Latin America]. Paper presented at the seminar "Women and Anthropology," Universidad de Chile, Santiago, March 1992.

Montecino, Sonia, Mariluz Dussuel, and Angélica Wilson. "Identidad femenina y modelo mariano en Chile" [Women's identity and Marian model in Chile]. In *Mundo de mujer: Continuidad y cambio* [Women's world: Continuity and change]. Santiago: CEM, 1988.

Morandé, Pedro. *Ritual y palabra: Aproximación a la religiosidad popular latinoamericano* [Ritual and word: An approximation to Latin American popular religiosity]. Lima: Centro Andino de Historia, 1980.

Olalquiaga, Celeste. "Cultura buitresca: El reciclaje de las imágenes en la postmodernidad" [Vulturesque culture: The recycling of images in postmodernity]. *Revista de crítica cultural* 6 (1992): 7–10.

Olea, Raquel. "Feminismo: Una utopía que tiene lugar" [Feminism: A utopia with a place]. Paper presented at the seminar "Modernidad/posmodernidad: Una encrucijada latinoamericana" [Modernity/postmodernity: A Latin American crossroads], organized by ILET (Instituto Latinoamericano de Estudios Transnacionales [Latin American Institute of Transnational Studies]), Buenos Aires, and the *Revista de crítica cultural*, Universidad de Chile, Santiago, May 1990.

———. "El lugar de Gabriela Mistral" [Situating Gabriela Mistral]. In *Una palabra cómplice: Encuentro con Gabriela Mistral* [The complicit word: An encounter with Gabriela Mistral], 17–19. Santiago: Isis Internacional, Casa de la Mujer La Morada, 1990.

————. "Más sobre mujer y escritura" [More on women and writing]. *La época: Literatura y libros*, 10 March 1991, 2–3.

————. "La redemocratización: Mujer, feminismo y política" [Redemocratization: Women, feminism, and politics]. *Revista de crítica cultural* 5 (1992): 30–32.

Olhagaray, Nestor. "Video Ready Made." *Margen* 4 (1985).

Ortega, Julio. *El discurso de la abundancia* [The discourse of abundance]. Caracas: Monte Avila, 1990.

Owens, Craig. "The Discourse of Others: Feminists and Postmodernism." In *The Anti-aesthetic: Essays on Postmodern Culture*, ed. Hal Foster, 57–82. Port Townsend, Wash.: Bay, 1983.

Oyarzún, Kemy. "Edipo, autogestión y producción textual: Notas sobre crítica literaria feminista" [Oedipus, autogestation, and textual production: Notes on feminist literary criticism]. In *Cultural and Historical Grounding for Hispanic and Luso-Brazilian Feminist Literary Criticism*, ed. Hernán Vidal, 587–623. Minneapolis: Institute for the Study of Ideologies and Literatures, 1989.

Perlongher, Nestor. "Avatares de los muchachos de la noche" [Incarnations of the boys of the night]. *Nueva sociedad* 109 (1990): 124–34.

Pollock, Griselda. *Vision and Difference: Femininity, Feminism, and Histories of Art*. London: Routledge, 1988.

Richard, Nelly. "Latinoamérica y la Postmodernidad" [Latin America and Postmodernity]. *Revista de crítica cultural* 3 (1991): 15–19.

————. *Margins and Institutions: A special issue of Art & Text* 21 (1986).

————. "El signo heterodoxo" [The heterodox sign]. *Nueva sociedad* 116 (1991): 102–11.

————, ed. "Cultura, política y democracia" [Culture, politics, and democracy]. *Revista de crítica cultural* 5 (1992).

Richard, Nelly, et al. *Arte en Chile desde 1973: Escena de avanzada y sociedad* [Art in Chile since 1973: Avanzada scene and society]. Document 46. Santiago: Flacso, 1987.

Rose, Jacqueline. *Sexuality in the Field of Vision*. London: Verso, 1986.

Rossanda, Rossana. "Nuestras perlas escondidas" [Our hidden pearls]. *Debate feminista* 2 (1990): 123–44.

Sabaj, Marcela. "Texto, cuerpo, mujer: A propósito de *El tono menor del deseo* de Pía Barros" [Text, body, woman: On Pía Barros's *El tono menor del deseo*]. *La época: Literatura y libros*, 24 November 1991, 3.

Said, Edward. "In the Shadow of the West: An Interview with Edward Said." In *Discourses: Conversations in Postmodern Art and Culture*, ed. Russell Ferguson et al., 95. New York: New Museum of Contemporary Art, 1990.

Sarlo, Beatriz. "Una mirada política: Defensa del partidismo en el arte" [A political view: In defense of partisanship in art]. *Punto de vista* 27 (1986): 1–4.

——. "Políticas culturales: Democracia e innovación" [Cultural politics: Democracy and innovation]. *Punto de vista* 32 (1988): 8–13.

Schopf, Federico. "Suplemento" [Supplement]. In *Poesía chilena de hoy: De Parra a nuestros días* [Chilean poetry of today: From Parra to our time], ed. Erwin Díaz, 20–30. Santiago: Ediciones Documentas, 1991.

Scott, Joan W. "Deconstructing Equality-versus-Difference; or, the Uses of Poststructuralist Theory for Feminism." *Feminist Studies* 14, 1 (1988): 33–50.

Soper, Kate. "Postmodernism and Its Discontents." *Feminist Review* 39 (1991): 97–108.

Subercaseaux, Bernardo. "Democratización y democracia cultural" [Democratization and cultural democracy]. *Revista de crítica cultural* 5 (1992): 27–29.

Toledo, Víctor. "Historia de la mujer en Chile: Historia de géneros: Apuntes para un balance preliminar" [History of women in Chile: A history of gender: Notes toward a preliminary account]. Paper presented at the seminar, "Women and Anthropology," Universidad de Chile, Santiago, March 1992.

Valdés, Adriana. "El espacio literario de la mujer en la colonia" [Colonial women's literary space]. In *Ver desde la mujer* [To see from the position of women], ed. Olga Grau, 83–105. Santiago: Ediciones La Morada, Editorial Cuarto Propio, 1992.

——. Paper on the book *Ver desde la mujer* at the Universidad Metropolitana, Santiago, August 1992.

——. "Una pregunta desde Chile" [A question posed from Chile]. FEM, November 1993.

Yúdice, George. "El conflicto de postmodernidades" [The conflict of postmodernities]. *Nuevo texto crítico* 7 (1991): 19–33.

Zurita, Raúl. "Ernesto Muñoz: The Last Star." In *Ruptura*. Santiago: Ediciones CADA, 1982.

Index

Adriasola, Teresa, 73 n.4
aesthetics, in art: and "art-system,"
    39–42; debate on, 31; feminine
    versus feminist, 29–30, 42;
    homosexual, 44–45, 49; of signs,
    29–42; television, 38; and use-
    lessness, themes of, 7. See also
    signs
alternative culture, sociology of, 7
"anticlassical" languages, 39–40
Arrate, Marina, 73 n.10
art: "bad image" in, 37; and cen-
    sorship, theme of, 33–34; during
    democratic reconstruction, 9;
    feminist theory and, 30–31;
    homosexual aesthetics in, 44–
    45, 49; and traditional left,
    5–6; transvestite metaphor in,
    47–48, 50–51; "unframing"
    in, 32; women's, 30. See also
    aesthetics, in art; transvestite
    metaphor
Art Actions Collective (Colec-
    tivo Acciones de Arte; CADA),
    71 n.10, 76 n.16
art exhibits, 30–31. See also specific
    exhibits

art history, and feminist theory,
    30–31
art scene, Chilean, 7
"art-system," 39–42
artists, Chilean women, 39–40. See
    also specific artists

"bad image," in art, 37
Bakhtin, Mikhail M., 72 n.19
Barbero, Jesús Martín, 70 n.1
Barret, Michéle, 79 n.14
"being a man," 22–23. See also
    masculinity
"being a woman," 22–23. See also
    femininity; "the feminine"
Berenguer, Carmen, 72 n.1
Beverley, John, 69 n.7
Bianchi, Soledad, 23, 73 n.6,
    74 n.16, 74 n.24, 77 n.10
body, in women's writing, 26–27
Boisier, Cecilia, 74 n.2
Breitling, Gisela, 76 n.13
Brito, Eugenia, 70 n.5, 73 n.2,
    73 n.4, 74 n.3, 75 n.5
Brunner, José Joaquín, 78 n.5
Buci-Glucksmann, Christine, 78
    n.6, 78 n.7

CADA (Colectivo Acciones de Arte), 71 n.10, 76 n.16
Camiruaga, Gloria, 38
Canclini, Néstor García, 78 n.5
Casas, Francisco, 49
censorship, in art, 33–34
Chilean art: and cultural scene, 7; versus literature, 41
Chilenas (Chilean women), 31, 74 n.2
Christ, Ronald, 75 n.4
Cixous, Hélène, 20, 73 n.11
clothing, and transvestites, 52–53. *See also* identity; transvestites
Congreso de Literatura Femenina Latinoamericana (International Conference on Latin American Women's Literature), 9, 17, 72 n.1
Contreras, Marta, 73 n.10
"crisis," of cultural authority, 60–61
criticism, cultural. *See* cultural criticism
criticism, feminist. *See* feminist criticism
criticism, literary. *See* literary criticism
crosses, images of, in art, 34
cultural authority, "crisis" of, 60–61
cultural change, forces of, 3
cultural criticism: and deviating practices, 2; and feminist theory, 1–16; function of, 1–2
cultural debate: critical junctures in, 3–8; and signs, 14; space for, television and press as, 4–5. *See also* signs
cultural ideologies, function of, 1
cultural scene, Chilean, 7
culture, alternative: sociology of, 7;

speaking through words and images, 1; and politics, dialogue between, 4–5

Dávila, Juan, 44–47, 77 n.1, 77 n.3, 77 n.9
debates. *See* specific topics of debate (*e.g.*, postmodernist, public)
de Certeau, Michel, 70 n.8
de Lauretis, Teresa, 76 n.17, 78 n.2
del Sarto, Ana, 69 n.5
democratic reconstruction, years of, art and literature in, 8–9
Derrida, Jacques, 63, 72 n.20, 79 n.15
deviating practices, and cultural criticism, 2
dictatorship: years of poetry in, 23; reflections on women during, 8
difference, gender: in art, 32; feminism of, 8, 61–67; and identity, 8; and feminist theory, 16, 24; in language and writing, 21; in postmodernist debate, 59; in poststructuralist debate, 65; types of, 62
disobedience, in art, 31–39
Donoso, Claudia, 77 n.11
Dussuel, Marieluz, 78 n.5

El Mercurio, 5, 33
Eltit, Diamela, 22, 28, 32, 74 n.2, 74 n.15, 74 n.17, 74 n.30, 77 n.12; and Círculo de Estudios de la Mujer, 73 n.4; and Círculo de la Mujer, 71 n.10; and Conference on Latin American Women's Literature, 72 n.1, 73 n.4; and Materiales de cámara, 75 n.7; and street actions, 36–37

homosexuality: First Meeting of Homosexuals (Primer Encuentro de Homosexuales), 51; in visual arts, 44. *See also* gay movement, in art; transvestite metaphor

Huyssen, Andreas, 65, 79 n.11, 79 n.20

"I": and feminism of difference, 62; and femininity, 66; in poetry, 23; and transvestite metaphor, 51. *See also* transvestite metaphor

identity: dissidence of, 22; of the feminine, 27; and feminism of difference, 63; fragmentation of, 64; and gender difference, 8; and "images of women," 20; of Latin American women, 15; in post-structuralist theory, 65; and the subject, 22–28; of transvestites, and clothing, 52–53; of women, 12; and women's art, 31

ideology: cultural, function of, 1; masculine-patriarchal, in Latin American context, 66

images: in art, 36; in media, 5; video, and Chilean women artists, 39; and words, culture speaking through, 1

"images of women," 19–20

Imbunches, 34

Infante, Macarena, 38

International Conference on Latin American Women's Literature (Congreso de Literatura Feminina Latinoamericana), 9, 17

Irigaray, Luce, 75 n.6

"irrational rationality," 57

journalism, feminine, traits of, 39

Kipnis, Laura, 79 n.8

Kirkwood, Julieta, 8, 15, 71 n.9, 72 n.21

knowledge systems, 14–16

Kristeva, Julia, 21, 74 n.27

Kuhn, Annette, 74 n.18

"Labor of love among the dwellers of a Santiago boardinghouse" *(Trabajo de amor con los asilados de la hospedería)*, 37

Laclau, Ernesto, 70 n.4

language: "anticlassical," and Chilean women artists, 39–40; gender difference in, 21; and identity of Latin American women, 15; in literary history, 25; masculinity of, 12–13; and radical feminism, 12–13; and signs, 14

Las Yeguas del Apocalipsis (The Mares of the Apocalypse), 49, 50

Latin American context, masculine-patriarchal ideology in, 66

Latin American feminism, and Euro-American theory, 58

Latin American modernity, and postmodernist debate, 57

left, traditional, and art, 5–6

Lemebel, Pedro, 49, 51, 77 n.15, 78 n.16, 78 n.18

Leppe, Carlos, 44–46, 77 n.3

literary criticism, on "the feminine," 19–20

literary history, and women, 24–25

literature, by women, 17–19; during democratic reconstruction, 9; gender representations in, 20;

posing, and transvestite metaphor, 47–48
post-coup, cultural context of, review of, 3
postmodernism: and cultural identity, 60; the feminine, 57–58; and feminism, 55–67; and modernity, Latin American, 57; and "the other," 61; and point of view, 56; and socialism, 7; and subject, 61; and Western-masculine representation, 60–61
poststructuralist theory, and identity, 65
power, in art, 31–39, 64
Pratt, Mary Louis, 76 n.*
Primer Encuentro de Homosexuales (First Meeting of Homosexuals), 51
prostitutes, portraits of, 48. See also transvestite metaphor
public space, for debate, 3–4

radical feminism, and language, 12–13
Rendell, Steven, 70 n.8
Renovación Socialista (Socialist Renewal), 7
"retouching," 46–47
Richard, Nelly, 69 n.2, 69 n.3, 69 n.4, 70 n.8, 74 n.2, 74 n.3; and Círculo de Estudios de la Mujer, 73 n.4; commentary on work of, 69 n.1; and Conference on Latin American Women's Literature, 72 n.1, 73 n.4; "gay" and "homosexual," use of terms, 76 n.†; travesti, use of term, 76 n.*; works in translation, 69 n.7
Riesco, Angela, 38

Rose, Jacqueline, 74 n.28
Rosenfeld, Lotty, 32, 34–35, 38, 71 n.10, 74 n.2, 75 n.7
Rossanda, Rossana, 11–12, 72 n.18, 72 n.24
Roudiez, Leon S., 74 n.14
Ruptura, 71 n.10, 76 n.16

Sabaj, Marcela, 19, 73 n.7, 73 n.8, 73 n.9
Sánchez, Cecilia, 73 n.4
San Miguel Hospital, Rosenfeld's art in, 35
Sarlo, Beatriz, 70 n.2, 76 n.11
Schopf, Federico, 74 n.21, 74 n.25
Scott, Joan W., 79 n.16, 79 n.17, 79 n.19
semantics. See language
sexual identity, and feminism, 27–28
signals of gender, and transvestites, 43
signs: aesthetics of, 29–42; in art, theme of, 31–39; and feminism of difference, 62; and language, 14; women as, 65
social change, forces of, 3
social identity, and feminism, 27–28
socialism, and postmodernism, 6–7
Socialist Renewal (Renovación Socialista), 7
social sciences, and art, 8–9
social thought, boundaries of, 2–3
sociology, of alternative culture, 7
Soper, Kate, 79 n.22, 79 n.23
space: in art, destructuring of, 35–36; public, for debate, 3–4
spatial politics, 1–16
Subercaseaux, Bernardo, 76 n.12

subject, the: "decentered," 61; and postmodernity, 60; "shattering" of, 27–28; and writing, 22–28
subjectivity: dissident, 42; theme of, 6, 66
symbolism of gender, in writing, 21

television: and aesthetics, 38; images in, 5, 39; as space for cultural debate, 4–5
theories. *See specific theories (e.g., feminist theory, poststructuralist theory)*
Toledo, Victor, 72 n.16
Trabajo de amor con los asilados de la hospederia (Labor of love among the dwellers of a Santiago boardinghouse), 37
transvestite metaphor, 45, 47–48, 50–51: and identity, 52; and names, 46; and photographs, 47–48
transvestites: identity of, and clothing, 52–53; images of, in art, 43–53; posing of, 50

Ulloa, Jessica, 38
"unframing" in art, 32
uselessness, aesthetic of, 7

Valdés, Adriana, 25, 72 n.15, 73 n.4, 74 n.19, 74 n.20, 74 n.22
video art, "bad image" in, 37
video images, and Chilean women artists, 39

Waller, Margaret, 74 n.14
"we," in feminine practice, 10
Western-masculine representation, and postmodernist debate, 60–61

Wilson, Angélica, 78 n.5
women: in Chilean art, 40–41; identity of, 12; images of, 39; literature by, 17; reflections on, during years of dictatorship, 8; subject of, public exposure of, 9
"Women, art and periphery" (*Mujer, arte y periferia*), 31, 74 n.2
women artists: North American, 39–41. *See also specific Chilean artists*
"Women in art" (*Mujeres en el arte*), 38
women's art, 30. *See also specific artists*
women's history, context of, 13
women's issues, in feminist practice, 11
women's literature. *See* writing, by women
women's voice, emergence of, 23–24
women writers: Chilean, 18; and feminism, 41; and "gender of text," 20; and minority writing, 26. *See also specific writers*
words and images, culture speaking through, 1
writers, Chilean women, 18
writing, by women: the body in, 26–27; gender of, 17–28; and history of literature, 24; and the subject, 22–28; symbolism of gender in, 21; versus "feminine writing," 18–22

Yúdice, George, 79 n.10

Zurita, Raúl, 23, 49, 77 n.14, 78 n.17

NELLY RICHARD is the founder and director of the journal *Revista de crítica cultural*, in Santiago, Chile. She is the author of *La estratificación de los márgenes: Sobre arte, cultura y política/s* (1989); *Masculino/femenino: Prácticas de la diferencia y cultura democrática* (1993); *La insubordinación de los signos: Cambio político, trans- formaciones culturales y poéticas de la crisis* (1994); *Residuos y metáforas: Ensayos de crítica cultural sobre el Chile de la transición* (1998). She edited *Políticas y estéticas de la memoria* (2000), and, with Alberto Moreiras, *Pensar en/la postdictadura* (2001).

SILVIA R. TANDECIARZ teaches Hispanic Studies at the College of William and Mary. A specialist in Southern Cone Cultural Studies, she has published articles on the relationship between Peronism and cultural production, feminist theory, and film. Her translations of theory and poetry have appeared in *South Atlantic Quarterly*, *Revista de crítica cultural*, and *Tameme*, and she published her first book of poetry, *Exorcismos*, in 2000.

ALICE A. NELSON teaches Latin American Cultural Studies and Spanish at the Evergreen State College. She has written extensively on contemporary Chilean culture, most recently, *Political Bodies: Gender, History, and the Struggle for Narrative Power in Recent Chilean Literature* (2002), and has published translations of short works by several Chilean authors, including Pía Barros, Soledad Bianchi, and Diamela Eltit.

LIBRARY OF CONGRESS CATALOGING-IN-PUBLICATION DATA
Richard, Nelly. [Masculino/femenino. English] Masculine/ feminine : practices of difference(s) / by Nelly Richard ; Silvia Tandeciarz and Alice A. Nelson, translators. p. cm.—(Post-contemporary interventions) (Latin America in translation/en traduccíon/em tradução) Includes bibliographical references and index. ISBN 0-8223-3302-3 (cloth : alk. paper)—ISBN 0-8223-3314-7 (pbk. : alk. paper) 1. Feminism—Chile. 2. Women in politics—Chile. I. Title. II. Series. III. Series: Latin America in translation/en traduccíon/em tradução HQ1547.R5313 2004 305.42'0983—dc22 2003018680